**Perestroika in India**

**V.P.Singh's**

**Prime Ministership**

VISHWANATH PRATAP SINGH

# Perestroika in India
# V.P.Singh's Prime Ministership

Edited with an introduction by

**G.S.Bhargava**

GIAN PUBLISHING HOUSE
New Delhi-110002

ISBN : 978-81-212-0330-2

Reprint 2019

*Published by*

GYAN

Gyan Publishing House
5, Ansari Road
Daryaganj, New Delhi-110002
Phone: 011-47034999, 9811692060
www.gyanbooks.com
E-mail: books@gyanbooks.com

*Printed at:* G. Print Process, Delhi.

# Contents

# *The Contributors*

**Nikhil Chakravartty,** a veteran journalist and a noted columnist is the editor of *Mainstream*. He is also President of the Editors Guild of India. His writings are noted for their freedom from prejudice and breadth of vision.

**N.S. Jagannathan,** a former editor of the *Financial Express*, specialises in writing on economic topics. He also contributes a column to the *Indian Express*. His approach to both political and economic problems is marked by freedom from dogma and a flair for freshness.

**Balraj Puri** has been a socialist activist in Jammu and Kashmir for over three decades. He brings to bear on his writings vision and understanding.

**George Mathew,** a social scientist is active in human rights organisations like the People's Union of Civil Liberties and Independent Initiative. He is also the Director of the Institute of Social Sciences, New Delhi.

**Devdutt** is a senior journalist associated with radical movements. A socialist by conviction, his political analysis combines historical depth with accent on principles.

**Sreedhar** is a senior research associate of the Institute for Defence Studies and Analyses, New Delhi, who has written extensively on security matters.

**Pradip Bose** is a writer and general secretary of the Indian Centre for Democratic Socialism, New Delhi.

**M.L. Ahuja** is a senior executive of a leading publishing organisation.

# Introduction

## Perestroika in India

Mikhail Gorbachev has made perestroika literally meaning restructuring - not only internationally popular but has also endowed it, perhaps unintentionally, with a revolutionary aura like socialism fifty years ago. It has come to be perceived as a modern version of the October Revolution in the Soviet Union which cannot be accomplished by lesser mortals like Vishwanath Pratap Singh and his colleagues in India. The reaction of some well-meaning friends to the title of this book has been to suggest that we are overdramatising and unduly glorifying the political change in India represented by the November 1989 general election to the Lok Sabha supplemented by the outcome of the February 1990 mini-general election to several State assemblies.

Even in the Soviet Union perestroika did not follow a revolutionary or violent upheaval, with or without bloodshed. It is the result of the emergence of one man - Gorbachev - at the helm of affairs in what has lately become a routine change of guard in the Soviet Union. Gorbachev's election as general secretary of the Soviet Communist party had neither the drama of Nikita Khrushchev stepping into Stalin's shoes nor the trauma of his deposition by his successors. It was a commonplace development, especially by Soviet standards. Yet the courage of convictions of the new leader his vision, determination and drive have wrought a revolution with reverberations all over the planet. The changes already undertaken by him - at home and abroad - and those in the offing are comparable in significance to the impact on the mind of man of the French and October revolutions put together. Human history has turned a new page, whether Gorbachev succeeds in accomplishing all that he has set out to or not. But at the root of the perestroika is a development no more extraordinary than a change in leadership through succession.

By the same token, the November 1989 general election in India has put "the crown of thorns" on a leader who has been striving to bring principles and values to bear on politics, which the people of India have not known for at least two decades. After Gandhiji's assassination and the eclipse of Nehru the idealist by Nehru the politician, the drift had started, which by 1980 gave rise to the description, "cesspool of politics." Here, as in Gorbachev's case, the accent is on the character and intentions of the leader and the qualitative change they will spell in the situation in India. The circumstances in which Vishwanath Pratap Singh has to struggle to make his dreams a reality are no less daunting than those facing Gorbachev in the Soviet Union. Perestroika refers to the effort--conscious, wilful effort--and not its likely result. He may be overwhelmed by the resistance to change in the system or may even be swept away by the forces he releases. Both the dangers are inherent in the Soviet situation also and there is no dearth of sceptics about the success of the Gorbachev revolution and Gorbachev's future itself. But they do not detract from the significance of the effort and its moral fallout. Further, as in the Soviet Union and elsewhere also, a single person at the helm of affairs, given vision and moral courage, can change the face of society. He or she is not a single swallow. It is so in every society and under any culture but more so in ours. Gandhiji and Jayaprakash are examples even if they did not fully live up to the people's expectations from them. They were not perfect but they were beacons on a new path.

Thus, the November 1989 general election in India is not a mere quinquennial event of the massive electorate exercising its franchise. It put an end to what was widely accepted as the unavoidable and permanent monopoly of power by a single party which ruled the country for 39 years of the 42 years of independence. The party acquired alphabetical suffixes, like "R" and "I", as it degenerated from a national platform for freedom struggle to a caucus of self-appointed chieftains. In the process, it came under the thrall of a single family, once revered and loved but ultimately discredited and devalued as a mother and sons company. When Rajiv Gandhi succeeded his mother as prime minister in late 1984, the tendency in both the west and the Soviet Union was that dynastic succession was an inherent aspect of Indian democracy. If Communist leaders like Nicolae Ceausescu and Kim Il Sung could bequeath power to their heirs so could a western type parliamentary democracy in Indian conditions. In fact, the monarchical trait was a source of political stability. Original thinkers like Girilal Jain had dinned into our ears that without the Congress party in power and without a member of the Nehru family in control of the party India would disintegrate. It was against that background that the Indian voter plumped for change. It is not merely a negative vote against Rajiv and his cohorts but a positive acceptance of the promise of perestroika with all its perils.

A venal aspect of the decay in the Indian political system is the calculated erosion of institutions meant to be pillars of the polity. In the ascending order of importance, the eroded institutions are the party system, parliament, the presidency, the judiciary, the press and the bureaucracy. The party was reduced to a personal fiefdom, without genuine membership, periodical organisational elections and an accountable hierarchy of leadership. A party with a popular base pumps new blood into the body politic. But the Congress party did not have organisational elections for over two decades because, it was said, there was no membership except in the formal sense. There was no membership because of the practice of fraudulent filling of forms or bogus membership as it is called. The phenomenon of ballot rigging in the shape of wholesale stamping of papers by outsiders is, incidentally, an offshoot of this. (Just as one does not go to the people to enrol them into the party similarly one does not canvass for support from the voters.) Still, since the formality of periodical elections has to be gone through, the "party" is turned into an election machine commanding all the tricks for garnering votes. When there are no elections, State power which the party monopolised is deployed in a sectarian manner to prolong the political life of the leaders. The State, the Government and the party became indistinguishable from one another. If a fraction of the country's precious resources expended on keeping the Congress party leaders and their hangers-on in the saddle in the last twenty years or so had gone into development the problem of poverty in India would not have been so acute. It seems from reports from eastern Europe that the Communist bureaucracies in several of those countries followed an almost identical method of self-perpetuation but the people, being more conscious and less inhibited by sectarian loyalties than us, got rid of them faster and in toto.

The Janata party in India tended to go the same way during 1977-79 when Chandra Shekhar and Madhu Limaye came down on enrolment of members and election of party functionaries on the alibi that the Jana Sangh constituent of the conglomerate would swamp the organisation and threaten the leaders' security of tenure. The party or what remained of it never recovered from the disability and had to make up for the weakness through blood transfusion in the shape of merger with other groups. The resultant Janata Dal could not understandably undertake party building during the last two years but it cannot be put off for ever. Vishwanath Pratap Singh's resignation from party presidentship, for whatever reason, is a right step. The party should grow as an alternate source of strength and a corrective, even if inconvenient at times. It will, of course, shine in the prime minister's reflected glory but should not be an adjunct of the State apparatus or a parallel establishment. Its sources of finance and other support should be autonomous as in many western European countries. In this context the danger of the Janata Dal emerging as a monolith is negligible. The clash of personalities among its leaders and the conflicting interests of its supporters will sustain plurality in the party even if they periodically yield juicy copy for political columnists. But such "revolts" and "rifts"-- as they are described in newspaper headlines -- are not destabilising in a democratic setup. Even in the Soviet Union inured to decades of dictatorship of the secretariat, Gorbachev allows dissent in the top echelons.

Another prophylactic against oligarchy under the new dispensation is that Vishwanath Pratap Singh and his team do not owe their position to any divine right or hereditary bequest. They are accountable. They have to reckon with diversity and dissent even if destructive sometimes. Neither the Indian State nor its political system is so fragile as to be "destabilised" (by disclosure of bribery by the Swedish radio or dissent in the ruling party) as made out by Rajiv Gandhi's apologists and their totalitarian mind-setters. We have survived in one piece twenty years of destructive rule. Thus, by its very nature, the dispensation under the Janata Dal will be heterogeneous and multifaceted. It will be governed by consensus and not conformity. At the same time, V.P. Singh and his colleagues should guard against the wholesale influx of Congress-I stalwarts in search of office. In the Janata Party of hallowed memory, Chandra Shekhar and Madhu Limaye kept open house for Dinesh Singhs, Raghuramaiahs and others to counter Atal Bihari Vajpayees and Lal Kishan Advanis of questionable secular credentials. While no mass party can shut its doors on entrants, large scale entry of stalwarts steeped in manipulative methods will not serve the party or the country. Nor will it be consolidation of any forces, centrist or noncentrist, even if it temporarily promotes factional interests.

There is, further, the unfolding multi-party scenario in the country. The Janata Dal, even with its partners in the National Front, is not India nor does it control the administration throughout the country. Even at the centre it is technically dependent on the support of the Bharatiya Janata Party (BJP) and the Communists, although in effect they have no option but to keep the Government going and going well. In other words, a multi-party system has come into operation, opening an era of coalitions, formal or otherwise. Notwithstanding the labels of the different parties and their claims, they are by and large regional in their sway, if not in outlook also in some cases. This is true of the Congress-I and the Janata Dal as well. How the Congress-I regains credibility, if at all, is its problem but it is obvious that its hold is limited to parts of south India, Maharashtra and the north-east. Similarly, the Communists, with the Marxists in the lead, have their pockets of strength in West Bengal, Tripura and Kerala, with a sprinkling of support in Bihar for the Communist Party of India. How the Communists will evolve in the light of the Soviet and east

European developments is an additional vanable in the situation. The Janata Dal strongholds are Uttar Pradesh, Bihar, Orissa and Gujarat, with the possibility of recovery in Karnataka. The BJP sphere of influence covers Himachal Pradesh, Delhi,, Madhya Pradesh and Rajasthan.

Then there are parties confined to single States like the National Conference in Kashmir, the Akalis in Punjab, the Asom Ganatantra Parishad in Assam, the Telugu Desam in Andhra Pradesh, the DMK and the AIADMK in Tamil Nadu and the Shiv Sena in Maharasthra. The mosaic is not immutable but the possibility of its reverting to a system of single party dominance is very, very remote. Even a two-party system is not on the horizon. The multiparty configuration will be promoted by the devaluation of ideology the world over. There is a remarkable convergence of one-time ideologies on a broad corpus of priorities and possibilities. Concepts like nationalisation of industry, class struggle profit motive in a *laissez-faire* way, vanguard or dominant role for a single party have all become cows shorn of their holiness. In other words, while a consensus on more and more issues is possible there is no corresponding shift towards centralisation of action. Such a situation will be conducive to a federal system to which the National Front is committed. Politics in the coming years will not be an extension of the State under a centralised control but will tend to be more and more autonomous and centrifugal in operation. There will be greater need for consensus politics in such a situation with labels like Right and Left losing their relevance. The youth, with its numerical preponderance in the population, will make itself felt bringing to bear on the agenda concern for the environment and the quality of life even while retaining its flair for material comfort and machine technology. (Incidentally, it has been overlooked that the lowering of the voting age in the election is also responsible for the rejection of Rajiv Gandhi and his caucus. The young men and women plumped for parties not regarded as progressive, whether in Maharashtra or backward Bihar.)

The Congress-I's assault on Parliament, the Presidency, the judiciary and the press and its subversion of the bureaucracy into a tool for partisan purposes is well documented. Not only were they sought to be emasculated directly but an indirect method of subornation was also employed. For instance, the Speaker of the Lok Sabha--third in the line of national succession--was an exalted officer of the State until Balram Jhakar discredited it by partisan conduct and collusion in shady transactions. The principle that the Speaker should be above party politics and should cease to be a member of a party even if elected on its ticket was given the go-by. His role in enabling the Bofors coverup by a parliamentary committee and his complicity in crippling the committees of parliament like the Public Accounts and Estimates Committees are other examples of his unworthy conduct. His very exit from the post has thus made a difference to its autonomy. Rabi Ray as the new Speaker has opened his account with an accent on fairness and probity. How Indira Gandhi and her son treated the Presidency, first by installing factotums in the high office and then by overriding them when they proved inconvenient are also well known. Shiv Shankar as law minister worked havoc with judicial independence and self-respect. There can be no worse indictment of the state of affairs than the Thakkar Commission report in which a judge of the Supreme Court allowed himself to be a instrument of factional feuds within the Congress-I establishment. The legislative enactments against the press on top of bending the law to harass independent newspapers and the buying up of journalists constitute Rajiv's record of media management. Today's ministers being parties to the resistance to these efforts are naturally opposed to them. The National Front is also committed to undo the evils and the Government has already moved in the direction by the proposal to establish a judicial commission to oversee appointment and transfer of High Court and Supreme Court judges and by withdrawing the law providing for tampering with the citizen's mail. The President is being treated with the respect due to the Head of State and has emerged as a key factor in building national consensus on controversial issues. More importantly, a tension-free atmosphere is conducive to the people asserting themselves against attempts to smother their rights. Unlike during the 1975-77 "emergency",the journalists developed the backbone to thwart the Rajiv Government's attempt to gag the press in the name of a law against defamation. The newspapers by and large functioned independently with the younger crop of journalists displaying healthy assertiveness. The bureaucracy is so massive that it cannot be controlled under a liberal dispensation like the present. In short as the institutions revive and begin to breathe freely the system will be resuscitated. This is a big step towards perestroika.

As important as the foregoing developments conducive to perestroika is the creation of an atmosphere in which problems can be considered rationally and a new thinking evolved for their solution. Gorbachev being a clearheaded dialectician has been able courageously to jettison dogma and advocate reforms unthinkable earlier. Starting with the ringing declaration that a war with nuclear weapons is unwinnable and should not be fought, he has propounded formulations which virtually rejected what passed for Marxism-Leninism earlier. He has also followed up his professions with bold actions at home and abroad. It is too much to expect any Indian leader, including V.P. Singh, to emulate the Soviet President in letter and spirit. But movement in the direction of drastic rethinking of policies is unavoidable for a perceptible change in the situation. It covers foreign policy including the safeguarding of national security as well as handling of domestic problems thrown up by civil unrest due to discord between religious communities. It will be a bad day for democracy if grievances, however legitimate, are sought to be ventilated through violence in the streets. It will erode the rule of law and force the Government, even if committed to pacific functioning, to embark on restoration of the public peace. Violence begets violence in an unending cycle of action and reaction. The cult has to be banished.

It is unfortunate, to say the least, that instead of allowing the National Front Government an opportunity to carry out its professions, the militants in Punjab and Kashmir are out to queer its pitch. It is as if there is a conspiracy to force the Government to follow in the footsteps of its predecessor. Despite the bold measures taken by the National Front Government to defuse the situation in Punjab and open a dialogue with all sections of the Akalis, the terrorist violence against innocent citizens is unabated. It is clear that the terrorists are afraid that the Government's commitment "to give peace a chance" in the State will make them redundant and are desperately bent on promoting strife. They have to be put down even if excesses are possible in the process. It was expected that the Akalis, especially the radicals among them, will distance themselves from the orgy of violence and force the terrorists into isolation. They have not shown the courage to do so. Whether it is now or months later, the Akalis' grievances and demands have to be sorted out through negotiations. A solution will not flow from the barrel of a gun. If the Akali leaders can summon up moral courage and statesmanship to displease the terrorists they will hasten the peace process. Otherwise, they will only prolong the situation in which the previous regime wallowed for years causing irreparable damage to the country.

The article heading this collection by one of India's most perspicacious political observers, Nikhil Chakravartty, brings out the convergence of both objective and subjective factors to facilitate government like that headed by Vishwanath Pratap Singh and to expect from it bold thinking and resolute action. We are really fortunate to have Nikhil-da in the small team of quite a few writers of distinction. Despite his high-minded idealism, he does not minimise the gravity of the situation on many fronts nor does he advocate short cuts to problem solving. For instance, he likens the situation in Kashmir to the problems posed to Gorbachev by the outlying Soviet republics - not to make the task look impossible but to underscore the possibility of its accomplishment by a Gorbachev-like approach. Balraj Puri's unemotional analysis of the factors which contributed to terrorist violence in Kashmir similarly points to what needs to be done and what is to be avoided.

George Mathew has brought out vividly the perceptions and problems of the minorities, especially the Muslims and the Christians. It is a cruel irony that with the physical security of the Muslims in such a parlous state an impression had been abroad among a large member of Hindus that reverse discrimination was being practised against them and that there was appeasement of the minorities. It shows how cynically the regime had exploited the Hindu-Muslim dichotomy for narrow party ends at the cost of national cohesion. The enactment of the Muslim Women's Protection Act overriding the Supreme Court decision in the Shah Bano case and the making of Urdu an official language in U.P. on the eve of the general election were glaring instances. While the former did positive harm to Muslim women and made it virtually impossible to think in terms of a uniform civil code, the latter was an insult to Urdu and a cheap gimmick to divert the Muslims' attention from the basic issues of security and identity. This raises the question of failure of the Muslim leadership and its propensity to make the Muslim voter a pawn in the power game. A secular ethos has to be created in which Hindus and Muslims do not act on sectarian lines except in the pursuit of their diverse faiths. This is a Herculean task but a beginning can be made. The distortion that has marred the concept of secularism has to be corrected so that the Muslims and other minorities are assured of physical security, equality of economic opportunity and denominational identity without causing misapprehensions among the Hindus.

The individual contributions in this collection bear the perspective of the writers. There is no common philosophy or theme overlaying them nor is the volume meant to project an organised school of thought. But the broad approach of most contributors is to re-examine the situation in the country in the light of the political changes and to relate the outcome to the need for fresh thinking for problem solving as well as the longer-term task of nation building. We see this as perestroika in India. But Devdutt, in his thoughtful article, adopts a larger framework of societal change and finds the new government wanting. He also questions the aptness of comparison with the Soviet situation on the misconceived assumption that we want Vishwanath Pratap Singh to play the sedulous ape to Gorbachev. The parallel is limited to breaking new ground, in thinking and action, not necessarily in policies and programmes.

M.L. Ahuja, a business executive, has wielded the pen to put forth what he calls the common man's view or *vox populi.* What is pejoratively called populism in India is perhaps the effort to win popularity by cosmetic changes but the common man's perception is luckily spared the epithet even if it may not be different in content. Governments have to evaluate people's needs and aspirations in terms of priorities and educate the people to put first things first.

Sreedhar is a talented representative of the vocal school of defence experts who advocate continuance, if not accentuation, of the past regime's unabashedly militarist approach to security in the region. His article graphically illustrates the phenomenon described in the joint paper by Pradip Bose and me of India being haunted by a spectre of insecurity in spite of unabated investment in the military. It glorifies concepts like "permanent adversaries" and "power projection" by India as a means of national cohesion and even sustained economic development. What Sreedhar dismisses as a low intensity conflict in Kashmir is now a grave threat to the country's security and territorial integrity. It did not emanate overnight from the National Front Government's pacifist professions and the consequent "wrong signals" to Pakistan and others. Nor is it the exclusive handiwok of Pakistan so that war psychosis vis-a-vis the neighbour will exorcise the demon from the Valley. It has arisen in spite of India's military strength and the presence of sizable troops in the State, exposing the chink in the armour of military-centred security policy. Military might will not be relevant to its solution except in the limited sense of putting down the terrorists and safeguarding the security of the people. The threat has to be overcome ultimately by political and other action which the previous regime had been unable even to visualise and, thanks to the experts' preoccupation with "defence preparedness" the country had been kept in the dark about the worsening situation until it burst on national awareness in the wake of the change-over. The formation of the National Front Government with its professed commitment to give peace a chance and its initiatives in Punjab might have prompted the terrorists to pre-empt similar moves in Kashmir. There could be no other provocation for the kidnapping of the Union Home Minister's unguarded daughter which is said to be contrary to both Islamic and Kashmiri traditions.

In Punjab also, but for the deployment of regular troops to storm the Golden Temple in 1983, the crisis would have been more manageable today. Similarly, Indian security had not been heightened by the use of the army, for long years, against our own nationals in Nagaland, Mizoram, Manipur and other areas in the north-east. In retrospect, it is now recognised that over-reliance on military means had delayed the assimilation of the mostly tribal people of these areas into the national mainstream. The attempt to rationalise Indian military involvement in Sri Lanka is more dangerous than fanciful. After a heavy cost in precious lives, of Indians and Sri Lankans, a severe drain on the Indian exchequer and avoidable erosion of the troops' morale, India is withdrawing its forces with the perceived threat to Sri Lanka's security unmitigated and the prospect of peace in the Tamil areas no better than in1987. Ironically enough, India-backed Tamils have now raised the cry of "eelam" in the north-east of the island. The problem has been discussed in depth in the joint paper.

The case against the militarist approach is not that the economy cannot bear the cost. If the security of the country demands military buildup and can only be secured thus there is no option. National security does not brook other considerations. But it is not so. That military spending is an engine of economic development is a dogma disproved in the Soviet Union and elsewhere. Whether what is called the peace dividend from cuts in wasteful and avoidable defence spending is an input in development or not, the perspective behind the change in emphasis is necessary to comprehend correctly the intensity of poverty among our people. Percentages are strategems to conceal the deprivation. The foregoing does not mean that India should live up to Gandhiji's dream of doing away with the military altogether. It is hoped that the proposed national security council will go to the root of the matter and help evolve a security policy in which the military is only a component. For over ten years now, the protagonists of the policy advocated by Sreedhar have had a field day– in the media and on the Government-run television and radio. Dissentient opinion hardly has its say. Still, the inclusion of Sreedhar's article in this collection is prompted by two considerations, apart from its professional merit. First, let the people judge after hearing both sides. Secondly, it should be a ready reckoner to the present government of the thinking behind the security policy all these years so that it can embark on bold thinking jettisoning the shibboleths.

Vishwanath Pratap Singh can give a new lead to the entire region by breaking away from the policy of competitive arms buildup and by going in for a mutual and balanced reduction of forces between India and Pakistan. That will aid the peace process and enable the two Governments to take problems like that in Kashmir in their diplomatic stride. The external affairs minister, Inder Kumar Gujral, has already set the correct style by ruling out war between India and Pakistan and some Pakistan leaders have reciprocated his sensible stand. In the larger sphere of relations with other neighbours also, India should steer clear of the temptation to pursue what is called a muscular foreign policy and live down the reputation of the Rajiv regime.

G.S.Bhargava

# *Vishwanath Pratap Singh*

## A Thumbnail Sketch

Paradoxical though it may sound, of all the prime ministers of India after Nehru, Rajiv Gandhi was the most highly rated at the start of his tenure. Lal Bahadur was an untested leader, diminutive both in stature and the expectations he aroused. Indira Gandhi was her father's daughter and the Syndicate's choice, and Morarji Desai rode to the position on the crest of Jayaprakash Narayan's charisma and leadership of the struggle against the "emergency"- although he never acknowledged it. The unelected prime minister, Chaudhary Charan Singh, who owed his elevation to manipulations in which the Head of the Indian State also had a hand, had been virtually robbed of his halo as a peasant leader by the circumstances in which he wangled the prime ministership.

But Rajiv from the word "go" was a shining star. He might have won the 1984 Lok Sabha election for his Congress-I party on a sympathy vote but his prime ministership was hailed by one and all who counted in a dispensation like ours. Dynastic succession to the leadership of a democratic polity – which was rightly anathema to the intelligentsia when his younger brother, Sanjay, was out to grab the position during the "emergency" – did not matter in 1984. Hard-nosed observers of the Indian political scene like Ramnath Goenka with over fifty years of active public life, academics of the stature of Myron Weiner of the Massachusetts Institute of Technology, and sworn adversaries of the ruling party like N.T. Rama Rao were all taken in by the Rajiv magic.

When he laid down the office in the dying weeks of 1989, Rajiv was perhaps the most despised of the prime ministers, including

Charan Singh. How he accomplished the miracle is not relevant here. What is germane is that prime ministers with larger than life ratings at the commencement of their terms end up differently. Against this background, Vishwanath Pratap Singh has a definite advantage which may do good to the country and himself. He is not seen as god's own choice to lead India in these difficult times. He has won a hard fought general election carrying on his shoulders a party which is a mixed bag of good, bad and indifferent elements. He has a mass base and the image of a good and decent person among the millions of Indians who deploy a sixth sense in judging their leaders unfazed by the exertions of professional image builders. More important still, he has no dearth of detractors who have raised a veritable industry of defamation and disinformation.

Being a good man is not a small qualification in any culture. The only advice Sir Walter Scott recived from his mentor on his death bed was "be a good man, my dear." The essence of the Hindu way of life is aspiring to be good men and women. The definition of goodness becomes more and more exacting as one delves into the dialectic, but the basic attributes are widely recognised. Sometimes, it is as simple as not being bad.

Vishwanath Pratap Singh's first exposure to the country at large was after the presentation of his budget in 1985. It was denounced as pro-rich by the so-called Leftists but the general reaction was favourable. Even those who did not understand the intricacies of finance and taxation were impressed, although they did not directly benefit from its provisions. More than that, they concluded that the finance minister was a good man, a compliment shared perhaps only by Chintaman Deshmukh and T.T. Krishnamachari among his predecessors.

Months later when what was derisively called "raid raj", meaning searches by investigators of the premises of suspected tax evaders, hit the newspaper headlines, the public added the adjective, 'decent', to its description of the finance minister. A powerful editor like Girilal Jain who had practically the entire Establishment with him, had read caste motives into the "raids", saying that they were motivated by the anti-bania bias of the Thakurs of whom Vishwanath Pratap Singh was one. Soon followed what was made a veritable inquisition of the veteran industrialist of Maharashtra, S.L. Kirloskar. Was it an act of vendetta or a sadistic exercise of power by Vishwanath Pratap Singh? I asked knowledgeable persons in Pune where I expected an explosion of anger against the humiliation of "the Henry Ford of Maharashtra". The answer was a "no", although some felt humanitarian considerations should have prevailed in respect of a person of such an advanced age. What was significant was that nobody doubted the motives of the then finance minister in ordering action against Kirloskar. In the light of the subsequent aborted action against businessmen close to the ruling family, like the Thapars and the Bachchans, V.P. Singh could not have spared Kirloskar. That he was thwarted in the later moves was a different matter.

I have highlighted Vishwanath Pratap Singh's relatively brief role as union finance minister because, first, it provided his first exposure nationwide, and secondly, because it was penultimate to his emergence as the *de facto* Leader of Opposition preparatory to assumption of prime ministership. According to his critics, Singh had craftily contrived to put himself in the position of a crusader against tax evasion with a view ultimately to challenging Rajiv Gandhi and replacing him. If it were so, Vishwanath Pratap Singh should rise in the estimation of political observers and the public as well because to be able to craft one's political career so meticulously and to anticipate the action-reaction cycle so precisely, one must be a Chanakya. But unfortunately, like many of his predecessors including Nehru and Lal Bahadur, Vishwanath Pratap Singh is not capable of such single-minded prosecution of his political fortunes.

It had been said of Indira Gandhi that as prime minister's daughter and hostess she had schemed to be Nehru's successor accepting Lal Bahadur as only a stop-gap diversion and had mapped out her strategy between 1962 and 1967. Some pundits had even credited Panditji with having wilfully promoted his daughter's ascent to the top-most position. Nehru might have

"emergency" by Indira Gandhi, which bade fair to do away with the democratic system in India. Birth in a well-to-do Thakur family owning the Daiya zamindari shielded him from the political and social currents afloat in the country as a result of Gandhiji's first non-cooperation movement. Vishwanath, as he was known until he entered politics nearly forty years later, led a sheltered life both as a child and as a teenager, left to indulge in his indoor hobbies of painting and photography. He is incidentally an ace photographer. The loneliness also led him to poetry, reading as well as writing, which meshed with his introvert nature.

The first break in the even tenor of his life was when as a graduate student at Allahabad University, he was drawn into student politics and fought and won the presidentship of the university students' union in 1948. A few years later he had similarly found himself involved in Acharya Vinoba Bhave's *bhoodan* movement. His friends and contemporaries coined the sobriquet, "V.N." - meaning Vishwanath - for him and not "V.P." or V.P. Singh as he is now addressed. Although I have no claim to first name familiarity with him, I have used Vishwanath in this sketch to lend informality to the narrative.

Later in 1957, Vishwanath Pratap Singh was attracted by the *bhoodan* movement as the culmination of a social service movement in which he had thrown himself heart and soul after completing his education. Almost on the spur of the moment, he donated a sizable plot of land in the Pasna village of Allahabad district as *bhoodan*. His traducers have been at pains to belittle and even distort the gesture saying, first, that his family, especially his wife, had remonstrated with Vishwanath for the "rash" act, and secondly, in the same breath, that it was a rocky piece of barren land. If it were so bereft of value or use, there would have been no reason for Vishwanath's relations to object to its donation. As it turned out, the donation was not the work of any sudden impulse because impetuosity is alien to him. He had thought about it and felt that he should join the *bhoodan* movement in deed rather than in words but he did not take his wife, Sita Kumari Devi, into confidence in the matter. Overriding objections from his family he stuck to his guns and never accepted the land back. Taking back a gift was against *dharma*, he maintained and gave it away to a college, Gopal Vidyalaya he had established at Koraon in Allahabad district.

Singh's upbringing was in an aristocratic environment which prevails to this day in most large landowning families of Uttar Pradesh even if the estates had dwindled or disappeared. To the people around him, he is still Raja Saheb, although Vishwanath personally dislikes the appellation. Scion of the zamindar of Daiya in eastern U.P., he was adopted at the age of five by the neighbouring raja or zamindar of Manda. While Vishwanath's own father Raja Bhagwati Prasad Singh, had four other sons by his two wives his adoptive father, Raja Ram Gopal Singh, was issueless. Being a consumptive, Ram Gopal Singh also kept his adopted son at a distance for fear of infecting him. Thus until Vishwanath was ten when his adoptive father died, he grew up in an atmosphere of loneliness except for a retinue of servants to attend on him.

A further complication was bad blood between the two zamindars. Vishwanath was forbidden from meeting his brothers or visiting Daiya. Because of threats to his life from rival claimants to the Manda zamindari, he was also constantly guarded by gunmen. It bred in his young mind an aversion for protection. His dislike for the security setup surrounding him as prime minister is apparently an off-shoot of the sequestered childhood, although he puts up with it due to the compulsions of the situation. After all, India cannot afford to leave its prime minister unguarded even if the precautions had been of no avail in Indira Gandhi's case.

After the death of his adoptive father, Vishwanath was sent to Colonel Brown's School in Dehra Dun a preparatory school for the pupils of the opulent. But instead of graduating to the Doon School which is often the second step from Colonel Brown's School, he joined the relatively plebeian Boys High School in Allahabad. Following a stint at the Uday Pratap College in Varanasi, again an exclusive institution for the education of Thakur youths, he entered the Allahabad University in 1948. Professor Murli Manohar Joshi of the BJP was among Vishwanath's lecturers at Allahabad and nurtured the younger man's flair for physics. Study of science fascinated Vishwanath so much that after taking a degree in law at Allahabad he went to Pune for an additional degree from Poona University.

Not having had to eke out a living from his degrees and not interested in taking to the practice of law, Vishwanath spent the first twenty years of his life looking upon studies as an end in themselves and pursuing subjects which interested him. In the process, he devloped an ethos which is both modern and traditional. Among the persons who influenced him most he lists Jayaprakash Narayan who epitomised the Socialist movement in the 1940s, Acharya Vinoba Bhave who spearheaded the Gandhian approach to public life and Lal Bahadur Shastri who was a product of the Congress practice of blending ethical values with the realities of competitive party politics. The result of such diverse influences in the formative years was not naturally a homogeneous philosophy. It is a mix of many factors. But its basic elements are rectitude, commitment to social justice and a moral dimension to politics.

1967 saw the Congress humbled at the hustings in many States. Dr. Ram Manohar Lohia's strategy of forging a broadbased united front against the Congress party and infighting within the party contributed to its loss of power in practically the whole of north India, from Haryana to Bihar. Defection became the political order of the day. Vishwanath was repulsed by the decay in political standards and would have perhaps stayed away from the political arena if his elder brother, Sant Bux Singh, had not influenced him in the opposite direction. The thinking then was that persons with commitment to policies and principles should enter politics and raise the tone of public life. Sant Bux Singh successfully contested the Lok Sabha election from Fatehpur, Vishwanath Pratap Singh's present constituency, and two years later prevailed upon Indira Gandhi to choose his younger brother as a candidate for the Vidhan Sabha election.

For two years Vishwanath remained a member of the U.P. Vidhan Sabha and was made the party chief whip later. While he did not set the Gomati on fire, he proved himself a conscientious legislator. Unlike the common run of MLAs, he did not specialise in distributing patronage but instead concentrated on attending to the grievances of his constitutents at large. As party chief whip, he had his eye on the implementation of professed policies, instead of limiting his labours to transfers and promotions of officials and upkeep of the "licence-permit raj." As he ruefully reflected later, it was, however, not enough if legislators were diligent and responsive to public needs. The organisation had to be dynamic with the infusion of new blood through periodical elections and the leadership would have to be concerned more about public welfare than fabricating an election machine. Indira Gandhi had neither the patience nor the genius for building a grassroots organisation as an instrument for the changes she professed. Her preoccupation was with entrenching herself in the State apparatus and using it for party purposes.

The associates she had chosen also did not have the capacity and courage to promote an organisational focus of power so essential in a developing country. The bitter experience of the Young Turks led by Chandra Shekhar and Mohan Dharia was proof of it. Critics of Vishwanath Pratap Singh have charged him with ingratitude and worse towards Hemvati Nandan Bahuguna who was said to have been instrumental in enabling him to enter the Lok Sabha in 1971. While it is unpleasant to talk ill of the dead, Bahuguna's *forte* was manipulative politics and not larger social and political purposes. His mercurial political career starting with his joining forces with Indira Gandhi at the time of the 1969 split, abandoning her on the eve of the 1977 general election, making up with his arch rival Charan Singh in 1979 to ditch the Janata Government and his subsequent walkover to the Congress-I, not to mention his later shift to the Lok Dal and founding a faction in it is proof of his temperament and political style. No wonder Vishwanath Pratap Singh could not keep him company.

Elected to the Lok Sabha in the 1971 "garibi hatao" wave Vishwanath bided his time until, in the wake of the Congress party reverses in the U.P. Vidhan Sabha elections, Indira Gandhi inducted him as a deputy minister in the Commerce Ministry in 1974. Almost two years later, he was made minister of state in the same ministry. He had thus remained with Indira Gandhi during the "emergency" even if as a mere cog in the machine. Apparently his concern for democratic rights of the people which is lately responsible in part for his break with Rajiv and the Congress-I was dormant in those days. The imposition of the "emergency" even without formal concurrence of the cabinet, the scrapping of fundamental rights including the right to life and the large-scale excesses in the implementation of the family planning programme and in putting down dissent had been clouded by the issue of Indira Gandhi's leadership and threats to it. Loyal partymen like Vishwanath did not look beyond the narrow groove in which even stalwarts like Kamalapati Tripathi and P.V. Narasimha Rao waded. Party loyalty has been a passion with Vishwanath even when it did not square with his other principles. When he resigned from the Rajiv Government in 1988, for instance, he was loath to quit the party because, first, he owed his membership of Parliament to it, and secondly, he hoped to fight for his principles from within the party.

The post-"emergency" Janata period accordingly found him in close company with Indira Gandhi and her rising son as Sanjay was called. He had even courted arrest in connection with the protests staged by the Congress-I against alleged persecution of Indira Gandhi by the Janata government. More recently, while handling dissensions in his Janata Dal party Vishwanath realised the danger of putting down dissent, even if motivated and unhealthy, in the name of enforcing party discipline. He realised that seeking unanimity and uniformity of opinion often resulted in the death of democracy itself, within an organisation or in the country at large. In his emotion-charged words, many a tomb of democracy carried the epitaph of unity. Thus, the last decade has seen a changed perspective in him on issues like the place of the individual in society and the supremacy of fundamental freedoms over what goes by the name of progress.

Re-elected to the Lok Sabha in January 1980, he was shunted off to Uttar Pradesh to head the State government barely seven months later. Indira Gandhi's style of shuffling persons from the

Centre to the States and *vice versa* to snuff out potential rivals to her and her heirs and as a way out of facing problems inherent in her leadership had started manifesting itself soon after her return to power in 1980. It was despite the convincing victory of her party in the 1980 Lok Sabha elections and virtual decapitation of the Janata as a party. Thus, even after the Congress-I had secured an absolute majority in the elections to the U.P. Vidhan Sabha she could not afford to let the party legislators choose their leader. Complicating the situation were Sanjay's own ministerial ambitions. On the advice of Kamalapati Tripathi, P.V. Narasimha Rao and other "elders", she decided against including Sanjay in her cabinet. So he had to be content to continue as an extra-constitutional centre of power, operating from his mother's drawing room along with R.K. Dhawan and "Brahmachariji". So, egged on by pals like Akbar Ahmed "Dumpy", Sanjay decided to be the chief minister of U.P. Accordingly the party was made to "elect" him as the leader. But it did not tally with Indira Gandhi's own calculations which required Sanjay to be by her side at the Centre – partly to keep an eye on his many-sided activities – and she got it nullified equally democratically. To fill the gap caused by the *denouement*, Vishwanath Pratap Singh was despatched to Lucknow to head the State government.

That Vishwanath had "readily" abided by the Leader's decision despite knowing full well that the Government of U.P. would in effect be run from New Delhi by Indira Gandhi, Sanjay and their myriad minions and that he would be left with responsibility without power speaks volumes of his sense of discipline and implicit faith in the Leader. In this respect he is like the boy who stood on the burning deck. He soon realised that his forebodings about the Lucknow assignment were well founded and began to look for an escape. His detractors' claim that he would go about in those days with the letter of resignation in his pocket was true, though not for the reasons adduced by them.

Communal violence which had become endemic to the State upset him most. There were charges of police excesses when the law and order machinery was allowed a free hand to deal with the trouble. Inquiries and admonitions in the wake of charges of police highhandedness demoralised the force and left them unequal to face organised groups of the rival communities, with hired goons in their tow, settling scores on one pretext or another. Basically, the "emergency" during which Sanjay and his followers had used the police with impunity for their own purposes - with the then chief minister Narain Dutt Tewari presiding over it in distant glory - and the street violence unleashed by the Congress-I to discredit and bring down the Janata Government had worked havoc with the law enforcement machinery. Violence was embedded in every protest, however legitimate. Land disputes and caste rivalry often erupted into massacres of the weak by the powerful because police protection, even if fail safe, could not be provided for every village and hamlet.

Vishwanath was disturbed beyond words by the phenomenon and thought "a moral shock" like the head of the Government owning responsibility for the incidents and resigning his post might work. But such a high-minded approach did not go well with Indira Gandhi's political calculations. She refused to let him quit after he had announced his resignation to the press. It not only embarrassed Singh but also brought into doubt the moral factor he tried to bring into play. So, following one more gruesome incident in June 1982, in which six Harijans were victims of an upper caste orgy at Mainpuri, he sent in his resignation direct to the Governor without waiting for the party president's permission. He was aware that in the process he had virtually burnt his political boats.

When he was drafted as chief minister in June 980 Vishwanath was not a member of the State legislature. He had been elected to the Lok Sabha earlier that year. So he vacated his Lok Sabha seat and was elected to the Vidhan Parishad to meet the requirement that a minister had to be a member of the legislature within six months of assumption of office. But chief ministers and prime ministers being members of the upper houses is an unhealthy practice because they will not be responsible to the directly elected lower houses. (C. Rajagopalachari in the undivided Madras Presidency and Morarji Desai in post-Independence Bombay State were members of their respective legislative councils as chief ministers of the States) Vishwanath, however, took the first opportunity of a by-election to enter the Vidhan Sabha in June 1981. Two years later, following his resignation as chief minister, he quit as an M.L.A. practically washing his hands of legislative politics in his home State.

Indira Gandhi again brought him in as union commerce minister, now with Cabinet rank, in January 1983, which necessitated his election to the Rajya Sabha through a by-election in July 1983. When Rajiv Gandhi entrusted him with the onerous finance portfolio on the last day of December 1984, he was a member of the Rajya Sabha. He remained so during the three years of his finance ministership, like his predecessor, Pranab Kumar Mukherjee, although the Santhanam Committee wanted prime ministers and ministers of finance to be members of the Lok Sabha. The irony is - as it happened in Vishwanath's case - that finance ministers cannot vote on their own budgets if they are not members of the Lower House. Incidentally, Indira Gandhi was not a member of the Lok Sabha during the first year of her prime ministership.

When Vishwanath resigned as defence minister in April 1987 after a three-month stint during which he ordered an equiry into payment of a hefty commission on the purchase of West German submarines - earning in the process the ire of Rajiv's sycophants - he also relinquished his membership of the Rajya Sabha. Fourteen months later, he was elected to the Lok Sabha from Allahabad in a by-election which was a turning point in the lives of both Rajiv Gandhi and himself. After that Vishwanath never looked back on his surging popular support and esteem, while Rajiv could not look forward to an escape from the web of deceit and corruption he had woven round himself.

The Lok Sabha by-election was caused by the resignation of the incumbent member, noted film actor Amitabh Bachchan who was indirectly implicated in the Bofors scandal. It was thought that Amitabh resigned his Lok Sabha seat to fight the resultant by-election and vindicate his claim of non-involvement in the Bofors payoffs - as V.K. Krishna Menon had done after he was indicted in the jeep scandal. But Amitabh simply disappeared from the political scene and his pal and patron, Rajiv, never cared to explain why Amitabh had originally entered the Lok Sabha and why he later quit under a cloud.

Expecting Amitabh to seek re-election, Vishwanath vowed to oppose him to test public opinion on the charges he had made against the Bachchan brothers of tax evasion and siphoning off slush money to Swiss banks. Rajiv's party which first boasted of fielding Amitabh again from Allahabad did not unveil its candidate until the last minute. When the "dark horse" happened to be Sunil Shastri - Lal Bahadur's son, and not Amitabh - Vishwanath was sought to be faulted for entering the contest even though Amitabh was not the Congress-I candidate. The significance of Vishwanath's pledge to contest against Amitabh either did not enter the heads of the Congress-I propagandists or they wanted to keep Vishwanath from the contest. The consequent membership of the Lok Sabha did not enhance his already high position on the political firmament. But winning the seat and forging a united front across the entire political spectrum in the process were politically significant.

Being an M.P. was also handy for Vishwanath in putting Rajiv and company in the dock on the Bofors bribes issue. He owned responsibility for the documents, some of which were already published by the *Hindu*, thus denying the government a loophole to ignore them on the alibi of their being "mere newspaper articles." (Incidentally, but for the enterprise and effort of the *Hindu*, the *Indian Express*, the *Statesman* and other newspapers, the Bofors issue would not have been the focus of public attention for well over two years.) The Government's response to Vishwanath's parliamentary initiative in the matter was the vilest abuse on him and his family. Buta Singh, K.K. Tewari, Vasant Sathe, Chidambaram and others had stooped so low that the proceedings in the Lok Sabha on that November (1988) day left a bitter taste in the mouth. Rajiv was prompting the disgraceful episode while Narasimha Rao and other elders did not have the moral courage to object. Even Krishna Chandra Pant whom I had respected until that day adopted the escapist stance of overlooking the evidence and trying to score debating points.

That virtually sealed Rajiv's political fate. More and more people were convinced of the complicity of the then prime minister in the crime. The delayed publication of the report of the Comptroller and Auditor-General, the personal attacks on the high functionary by senior M.Ps. like N.K.P. Salve and the resignation *en bloc* of the Opposition M.P.s from the Lok Sabha hastened the pace of the political change which had been triggered largely on the issue of honesty in public life. Judged by that yardstick alone, Vishwanath was the outright winner in the people's judgment.

Thus, Vishwanath's three main sources of strength are goodness, decency and honesty - as acknowledged by the people themselves - and not merely the parliamentary support of friendly parties backing the National Front government. The availability of this immense resource is an asset which distinguishes Vishwanath from both his former leaders, Indira Gandhi and Rajiv. They were in the red on that score. Lal Bahadur had no time to develop the moral dimension of his personality while Morarji Desai specialised in shrouding it with sanctimoniousness. Nehru had no need to draw on it because he was Gandhiji's political heir and often conducted himself as one. Thus, Vishwanath is unique among the prime ministers of India so far and the country expects him to live up to that position.

As earlier, Vishwanath's memberrship of the eighth Lok Sabha lasted for just over a year. He was elected in June 1988 and resigned as M.P. in July 1989. In fact, he has often shortened his legislative term voluntarily through resignation, both in his home State of Uttar Pradesh and at the Centre. The 1971-77 period was the only exception during which he remained a member of the Lok Sabha and served as a junior minister in the commerce ministry. Even his Rajya Sabha innings were a little short of the regular six-year span. The "Mahatmic" trait of punishing himself for system shortcomings is strong in Vishwanath. It is useful as a moral force but can also be destructive.

Finally, June has been an eventful month in Vishwanath's career. Born in June, he was married in June, became chief minister of U.P. in June and quit it in June two years later. He had also won the crucial Allahabad by-election to the Lok Sabha in June. June being the sixth month of the year is said to stand for being "middle of the road" and even-handed. It is a month of joy in most parts of the world, although not in Delhi. Above all, as the poet said,

"And what is so rare as a day in June?
Then, if ever, come perfect days."

G.S.B.

# 1

## *The Agenda*

**Nikhil Chakravartty**

After the ordeal of having to go through virtually two general elections in less than a hundred days, the National Front government under the stewardship of Vishwanath Pratap Singh can certainly claim to have earned a reasonable measure of durability for itself.

Right from the beginning, its supporters and detractors called it a "minority government" which in strictly parliamentary parlance, is a contradiction in terms – for no minority can really form a government in a system of democratic functioning. What has really been the state of things is that the biggest single party in the Lok Sabha has been so bereft of allies that it could not muster sufficient strength in the Lower House to lay claim to majority support to enable it to form a government. On the other hand, the three major formations in the Opposition joined hands to claim a comfortable majority; the fact of the matter is that of these three parties, the largest, that is the Janata Dal-led National Front has undertaken to shoulder the responsibility of running the executive, while the other two, namely the BJP and the Left, have preferred to stay out of government but have chosen to support it from outside. For all practical purposes, the National Front government is run on the basis of consensus among the three.

Such an arrangement has been made possible because of both the objective condition and the subjective factor involved in it. The objective condition underlying the present government is that the two allies – the BJP and the Left -- are equally dead set, if not more, to fight to keep the Congress-I out of power, and for that they, all three of them, are prepared to make utmost adjustments, mainly to keep the Congress-I out of power. Although between themselves, the BJP and the Left, have sharp differences - each denouncing the other as pernicious - they have identified their common concern to keep the Rajiv Congress out of power. It is this realisation on the part of both that has enabled the Janata Dal to take the initiative of forming and now running the present government at the Centre with the support of both.

Apart from this objective reality, the subjective factor which has kept the present government going is to be found in the importance of the personality of Vishwanath Pratap Singh himself. The manner in which he conducts himself, patiently seeking consensus on every major issue as also his personal traits which endear him to the native-born -- as distinct from the touch of the *feringi* burra sahib that characterised his predecessor in office - both have contributed in no small measure to the building up of the current three-party understanding which provides the foundation on which the present government stands. It is difficult to spot any other important personality today in our national life who can command such widespread support both in political circles and the public at large. This is a case of a political personality who has grown into leadership as he faced challenges and surmounted them. From the chief minister of Uttar Pradesh to the prime minister of India, Vishwanath Pratap has traversed rough terrain and at every stage has gained in leadership stature to the point that he is today the tallest in his party and a unifying factor in national politics.

It is in this context that one has to examine the major tasks that face him, the tasks that have to deal with the major problems facing the nation. What then is the predominant question facing our national life today?

All over the world today, political life has come under severe scrutiny -- a wave of rethinking has overtaken the leaders and parties in many countries. It will be incorrect to think that this urge for reappraisal is evident only in the communist countries. It is to be noticed even in the extreme conservative camp. The release of Nelson Mandela by itself does not mean the end of apartheid. The struggle against racial discrimination shall of course go on. At the same time, one has to acknowledge that a certain measure of rethinking has taken place even within the cooped up vault of the Pretoria regime. One discerns in the USA signs of serious rethinking on diverse issues -- from defence spending to social service demands, to assertion of Black rights - in other words, perceptible uneasiness at holding on to the status quo. The challenges of the cold war are being replaced by the need for response to the opening up of Moscow's totalitarian world. In other words, perestroika, the urge behind that movement, has ceased to be a monopoly of Gorbachev's Russia.

In such a world of breath-taking changes, how can India cling on to old concepts, old strategies or old policies in any department of human activity? One of the formidable tasks before the present government is to reshape the economic strategy. What new direction to be given to the economic policy, what new approach to tackle the besetting economic problems, can by no means be relegated as the exclusive concern of the finance minister and his officials: it has to be the concern of the entire government, of the ruling party transmitting it to the nation as a whole. On the question of approach to economic problems, there has already come up certain divergence in outlook between the report of the prime minister's economic advisory committee chaired by Professor Sukhomoy Chakravarty, and the deliberations on the draft of the Eighth Plan prepared by the newly constituted Planning Commission under the stewardship of Ramakrishna Hegde. Such divergences are to be welcomed - more the discussion the better for re-designing the economic strategy of the nation. In fact, rethinking and redesigning are over-due, because the experience of the last four decades has shown that while we have registered economic growth, the commitment to social justice has received far less consideration than the aspect of the growth in our planning. This debate started more than ten years ago and it is time it is taken up in all seriousness. This has become necessary because traditional thinking on economic strategy is being assailed practically all over the world and we cannot afford to remain in a state o intellectual autarky.

Major challenges from within the country face the present government. Practically all of them are legacies inherited by it. The Punjab crisis, for instance, has been with us for the last seven years. Indira Gandhi treated it on an adhoc basis, assailed as she was by contrary pulls within her government while she herself never bothered, particularly in the last phase of her regime, to work out a well-thought out strategy to deal with the question posed by armed militancy of Sikh extremism, a negligence which led to the desperate step of the Operation Bluestar for which she had to pay with her life. Rajiv with his penchant for flamboyance had in the first round signed the accord with Longowal, followed almost immediately by the election to instal the Akali ministry under Barnala, while he did not bother to honour the Longowal accord - not even to try the guilty of the November 1984 Sikh pogrom in Delhi. The dismissal of the Barnala Ministry came on the plea of its failure to curb terrorism, though the spurt of killings shot up under the President's rule. The prisoners were released in driblets while new conspiracy charges were cynically framed against those whom Rajiv himself had to release later, as if he held the power of life and death over anybody he disliked or found intractable. In the final analysis, there was total anarchy in policy perspective on Punjab on the part of Rajiv Gandhi.

Much the same story has been repeated with regard to Kashmir. Under Rajiv, things went from bad to worse and as a desperate measure, he struck an alliance with the same Farooq Abdullah and his National Conference whom his mother had dislodged from power out of sheer petulance, and to which Rajiv at that time installed as a Congress-I bigwig, had subscribed. But the alliance with Farooq was only an entente at the level of leadership without there being any serious rapport between the two parties, the Congress-I and the National Conference. The coalition ministry that was set up became only a den of corruption and maladministration earning the almost universal antipathy of the public in the State. The centre did nothing to guide or pull up the State Ministry because Farooq has been Rajiv's pal, belonging to the same tribe of political profligates. The result has been that the elements demanding secession have got the upper hand. There are of course differences within the camp of the anti-India elements - those who want Kashmir to be annexed to Pakistan and those who want an independent Kashmir. However, the discredited coalition of the National Conference and Congress-I was in no position to politically intervene in this critical situation.

For both Punjab and Kashmir, Vishwanath Pratap Singh and his Cabinet colleagues will have to do severe reappraisal. They will make no headway by just taking some palliative measures: it has to be a thorough reappraisal, to be followed by bold decisions courageously implemented. It will not do to get stuck over the controversy round Article 370 for Kashmir : one has to go very far beyond. To retain the Valley of Kashmir within the Indian Union today is not by any means easier than the unrest in the fringe republics of the Soviet Union. The choice has to be boldly and squarely placed before the people of India. In Punjab too, the niggardly negotiations with some well-meaning Akali leaders will take V.P. Singh nowhere. How to meet the militants and through whom, are the questions demanding immediate consideration.

In the wider canvas, there are urgent regional problems waiting to be tackled. These are more complex than being lumped together under the category of the Centre-State relations. Whether it is the question of Jharkand, or the tribal aspirations in the north-east from Bodo to the Mizo, these can no longer be shelved nor can they be dealt with compartmentally or passed on to the State Governments. New forms of approach, new structures have to be thought out if one has to expect any enduring solution.

As for the relations between the Centre and the States, the V.P. Singh Government has of course taken a correct decision to set up the Inter-State Council as envisaged in the Constitution. But this is not just a matter of structural maladjustments. There has to be a change in the basic understanding on the question of the role of the States and the Centre for the smooth and just functioning of our democracy. Decentralisation, panchayati raj are reduced to mere cliches without any serious attempt at readjusting the mental horizon of the politician or the public.

Bold thinking has become imperative in dealing with the entire question of India's cultural matrix. With this is interlinked the entire question of communalism. Although the conventional school of thinking would say that the appearance of the BJP at the centre-stage of Indian politics would make it more difficult to curb communalism, one would like to point out that with ascendancy of the BJP in parliamentary politics, one would be warranted to expect that over the years, the BJP interested in the politics of power would have to emerge as a nationally accepted political entity, and like the Communists, would be shedding some of its sectarian attitudes, that is it has to subscribe to the imperatives of the nation's composite culture. No doubt this is going to be a difficult task, but Vishwanath Pratap Singh and his establishment are better placed to undertake it as they have already established a political rapport with the BJP.

There has to be new and unorthodox explorings into the urgent question of making the entire nation literate. When Rajiv Gandhi talked of a new education policy, one had expected that top priority would be given to the task of universal literacy. Instead came the new fangled scheme of Navodaya Schools which have eaten up resources without bringing in corresponding returns. It is for the V.P. Singh Ministry to bring this urgent national task back to the rails and take up the question of literacy as of immediate urgency that must involve all concerned, both the Centre and the States.

In the sphere of foreign affairs, there is need, very urgent need, for rethinking. The traditional approach to problems will no longer work, nor can one go on repeating the age -- old cliche of being friendly to both superpowers. What we have to take into account today is not just the end of the cold war between the two super powers, but the appearance of more superpowers–hi-tech economic superpowers, namely Japan and Germany. The emergence of an integrated Europe has to receive our priority attention if we have to modernise our economy without jeopardising our commitment to self-reliance. A self-reliant approach will not only be a guarantee of safeguarding our independence but will also provide fresh impetus to our own advance towards being a major power in the emerging world of technology.

Within this framework, we have to establish close rapport with our neighbours, overcoming decade-long prejudices and angularities that beset our approach in the past. Indo-Pakistan relations have long remained a hang-over of our searing experience of the partition. More than forty years from then with a new generation in the saddle, must we not think in fresh terms? And the initiative for fresh thinking not only with regard to Pakistan, but with regard to Sri Lanka, Nepal, Bangladesh has to come from India as the biggest of them all.

It is India which has to be the pace-setter in South Asia, and it is up to Vishwanath Pratap Singh and his colleagues to boldly initiate new thinking on that score. The people of India beckons the leadership to go forward with courage. Let mistakes be made in this adventure: they are part of the adventure itself. But to wallow in the old-groove outlook will lead to a dreary dead end for this great nation, and disaster for the leadership thrown up by the trusting millions of this country.

Here lies the real agenda for Vishwanath Pratap Singh if he has to be true to the trust reposed in him by the forces of history.

# 2

## *The Economic Outlook*

N.S. Jagannathan

Any discussion of the outlook for the Indian economy in the wake of assumption of power by the National Front under the leadership of V.P. Singh should take into account four contextual factors. First, India is in the midst of a momentous political transition: old stereotypes are crumbling all too obviously but the contours of the new formations are far from firmly set or even clearly outlined. After 43 years of single party government at the Centre of which the Congress was in power for forty years in two phases--we have for the first time a coalition government in Delhi. Whether this presages an era of coalition politics is too early to say, though the very fact of the once unthinkable idea being a reality may well suggest that things will never be the same again. It is true that this new coalition is fragile and could collapse the moment either the BJP or the CPI (M) decides to ditch it. But the fact that both these parties, carrying on a phoney ideological war between themselves, have committed themselves to keeping the National Front Government going is clear evidence that a coalition temper is very much in operation. Ancient shibboleths have lost some of their vigour and there is a distinct possibility of a wider coalition in the years to come.

In this sense, the decisive break with the past did not occur in 1977 when the Congress monopoly of power at the Centre was ended by the Janata Party being voted to power with an absolute majority in Parliament but in 1989. From the point of view of economic management a climate of coalition politics will determine the nature of the tensions and compromises that shape policy and its implementation.

Secondly, this transition in India is taking place at a time when profound--indeed revolutionary--shifts are occurring all over the world in thinking about political and economic structures. Long in maturation, these changes have found dramatic expression in the eighties, first in Poland and Hungary, then in the Soviet Union and later in the rest of eastern Europe. These changes are as decisive as the French or the Russian revolution and their consequences will unfold themselves in the coming decades.

Elsewhere, less dramatically but nonetheless effectively, received "socialist" doctrine has been on the retreat in Britain and some other countries. Some of the consequences of this lesser revolution have been harsh, ugly and regressive. Indeed they have longed to destroy many of the ineffable virtues of compassion and social concern by selfconsciously promoting some of the nastier instincts of early capitalism. But these changes have gained political and social sanctions in many countries that had earlier embraced socialism with some ardour. This shows the exhaustion of once vital ideas either by fulfilment or by obsolescence by collateral developments in technology and social mores. These changes in perspectives may not be directly or wholly transferable to India. But their "demonstration effect" cannot be underestimated.

The third relevant fact is that no government has a clean slate to write its own special agenda. There are established continuities and asset structures that cannot and need not be dismantled. The Indian economy is not what it was forty years and even ten years ago. There certainly is need for evolving a new development strategy but the need for this arises as much for removing the distortions that have developed in the economy as from the new opportunities created by earlier efforts.

Not all that has happened in the last forty years can be fairly described as detrimental to the well being of the people or as enfeebling the economic strength of the nation. Arguably, an alternative model might have produced better results, especially in terms of social development rather than of economic growth. But the results of the strategy so far followed--which itself might not have been pursued in all its rigour and therefore produced unintended results--are not easily reversible even if one were inclined for good and bad reasons to attempt to reverse them.

In some ways the new directions are made possible by the very fulfilment of some of the old objectives. For example, the emphasis on heavy industry and infrastructural development has created, at perhaps excessive economic and social cost, an industrial structure that makes easier a strategy of industrialisation with emphasis on the production of wage goods and employment generation. In any case, any rational strategy for the future cannot afford to waste by desuetude the assets already in position. Indeed, further investments in power and similar areas have to be made if only because they are necessary to underpin the new strategy.

The fourth consideration that would necessarily govern economic decision-making by the new government is the conflict between short and long term objectives. This is in some ways the most serious constraint on the new government's desire to fashion an economic strategy after its own heart's desire and intellectual conviction. There are three facets to this predicament. First, there is the "fire-fighting aspect" of having to deal with certain immediate problems inherited from the previous government.

Secondly, highly desirable long-term structural reforms not only take time in yielding visible results but cause immediate dislocation and distress not only to the entrenched interests sought to be dislodged but also to the eventual beneficiaries of the reform. And this leads to protests--and this is the third problem--from those affected in various degrees and varying political clout. Coping politically with these protests in a situation of competitive politics becomes more important than the pursuit of the reforms themselves. It is a bind that Gorbachev is feeling most acutely. In India, which is an articulate and in some ways anarchic democracy, the problem is particularly acute. And for a minority government, itself a coalition and dependent on other parties for mere survival, the path of reform is going to be full of thorns and boulders.

A further complication is that the different constituents of the national government and even different members of the Janata Dal, the major constituent in the coalition, have different perceptions about the nature of the economic problems and contradictory approaches to their solution. These and the differing attitudes of the supporters from outside of the National Front may generate tensions of various sorts. But, paradoxically, the very necessity to survive might make for emphasis on policies and approaches that unite rather than that which divide. This is all the easier because there is a surprising degree of commonalty on details in the manifestoes of the parties, though being political documents their internal consistency is extremely tenuous.

Against this background, one can discuss the immediate and medium term objectives of the new government.

First, the short term outlook: The three major areas of concern are the parlous state of the finances of the government as indicated by chronic budgetary deficits, mounting inflationary pressures on the economy, partly the result of these deficits and the grave external payments situation. The Economic Advisory Council (EAC) headed by Dr Sukhamoy Chakravarti--incidentally the creation of the previous government--has succinctly summarised the inheritance of the new government from the old thus:

> The decade of the eighties has seen a period of relatively high growth of the Gross Domestic Product (GDP) at around five per cent per annum, which compares favourably with that recorded by most developing countries. Yet, the pattern of growth, methods of financing employed, both internal and external, have been such that, at the end of the decade, it

would appear that the strategy of growth pursued, especially over the last five years, needs some crucial modifications, if growth with self-reliance and equity remains the central focus government policy. This is because the contradictions inherent in the strategy have surfaced very starkly of late and will not go away on their own. While there remain certain areas of strength--the resilience of the economy in the face of weather stress, the buoyant climate for industrial investment, the rapid growth in exports, especially during the last three years improvement in some areas of infrastructure--these are not enough by themselves to ensure that growth can continue in the same way as before without generating either more inflation or even greater pressure on the balance of payments.

The basic imperatives stemming from the current economic situation would require the country to concentrate on removing fiscal imbalance, greater efficiency in the utilisation of existing assets, import rationalisation and export expansion in high value added areas. Management of the price line would require, in addition to above measures, certain supply side adjustments affecting availability of essential wage goods. In the medium term context, what the country should aim is to devise a strategy that concentrates on a broad-based growth pattern with adequate emphasis on removing disparities between sections of the population and regions rather than aim at a higher rate of growth in aggregate output than was achieved in the seventh plan.

In other words, the energies of the new government, especially the finance minister, would be directed in the next twelve months not so much to the long-term tasks of reshaping the economy on a different strategy--though these will have to be articulated and debated--but on restoring some semblance of solvency to government finances, getting the better of inflationary pressures and controlling the growth of imbalances in external payments.

The desperateness of the fiscal situation does not have to be argued at length. For the past several years, the budgetary deficit of the central government has been well over Rs 5,000 crores, a figure that would have scandalised earlier generations of fiscal managers. According to the latest official estimates, short term borrowing of the central government from the Reserve Bank of India at the end of December 1989 stood at Rs 11,800 crores as against Rs 8,600 crores at the end of December 1988. This is to be set against the estimate of the budgetary deficit made last February by S.B. Chavan, the then finance minister, of Rs 7,337 crores. The last quarter of the financial year may witness a spurt in tax and other receipts. There could also be a staggering of the budgeted spending to spill over to the next year, though this may not result in any substantial reduction of the amount scheduled to be spent. It is in any case extremely unlikely that the actual deficit at the end of year will be less than that projected in the budget last February. When Madhu Dandavate presents his budget in March, he will have to give the first indication of the government's resolve to contain the runaway spending that has been built into the system in the last ten years. This will be the first priority of the new government.

The Economic Advisory Council has repeated familiar counsel, based on the even more familiar disaggregation of the total spending of the government into four broad heads of defence outlay, interest payments, subsidies and general housekeeping costs of the government. On defence spending, the EAC is rather unrealistically suggesting that the reduction in global tensions and improved relations with our neighbours would enable cuts. This may have some validity as a long term projection but not as a determinant of the coming year's outlay on defence. However, spending on defence is one of the most opaque areas of our public finance, with the "mantra" of security risks being routinely used to ward off any rational scrutiny.

Interest payments which have been growing in volume over the years stem from the tendency to resort to the relatively painless mode of raising resources in preference to the more demanding mode of taxation. Clearly, with increases in the rates of interest in recent years, there is an element of illusion in this mode of resource mobilisation since a progressively larger part of the sums borrowed is being eaten up by the interest paid. Though we have not come to the desperate straits of having to borrow merely to pay interest, in recent years capital receipts are financing revenue deficits. This trend was supposed to have been reversed by Chavan in the current year's budget by his estimation of a modest revenue surplus. (This miracle was achieved by a fiscal sleight of hand that orthodox public financial experts would have frowned upon.) But even this estimate has been overtaken by events and we may well end up with a revenue deficit.

On subsidies, though there is enormous scope for rationalisation and reduction, the interest groups represented in the Government are hardly likely to permit any significant cuts. A government committed to the write-off of loans to farmers, higher support price--indexed for inflation--for produce, is hardly likely to seek to reduce subsidies on fertiliser, electricity and water. Similarly consumer subsidisation of grain and so on through fair price shops can at best be nibbled at the edges. But this will be neutralised by the very necessary extension of the public distribution system to the really vulnerable in the rural areas neglected so far. Still some savings can and should be made by what the EAC calls "better targeting" of beneficiaries by the introduction of a "means test" for eligibility for subsidised supply of basic commodities.

One way to really get to grips with the problem of government spending is not to look for economies by wholesale jettisoning or reductions in broad heads of spending (which really means throwing up your hands in despair) but to submit every item, no matter under what head--development or non-development, plan or non-plan--to the strictest scrutiny of necessity and cost effectiveness.

Extravaganzas like "utsavs" and festivals that the Rajiv Government indulged in would automatically fail this test. Less visible is the waste involved in the loose budgeting and monitoring of the so-called project and programme spending under the plan, where cost and time over-runs, leakages, corruption and swindles are quite common, as successive CAG and Parliamentary committee reports have highlighted. A mechanism must be devised for contemporaneous monitoring of such spending instead of *post facto* scrutiny by the CAG, who in any case cannot look into anything more than a fraction of government spending.

By tradition and habit, the receipts side of a budget receives more detailed public discussion than the expenditure side. Tax proposals and public borrowing have interesting technical aspects, whereas spending has no such facets, except for the bureaucrat who knows his ropes and who would much rather keep his knowledge to himself. Perhaps an Expenditure Commission such as the one set up by Charan Singh in his short tenure as Prime Minister and which was promptly abolished by Indira Gandhi soon after she assumed office is worth revival, if only to get a measure of the problem.

Finally, the only real solution for the problem of deficit is to get the public sector units to generate the surpluses expected from them when they were set up. Successive plan documents have routinely assumed a certain order of resources generated by these units for the financing of the plan investment. Though individual units have produced surpluses at least as internally available resources for their own use–some of them have also paid dividends to the general exchequer–the public sector as a whole has never generated the assumed resources. There is thus a direct correlation between the shortfall in the assumed surpluses of the public sector and the excess of deficit financing over the figure assumed in the plan, whenever the plan outlay is fully spent.

Of course this is a simplistic correlation.

It does not take note of inflationary erosion of funds provided at the base year's prices. The assumed surpluses from revenues at existing rates of taxation also do not materialise. But, as a working proposition, it could be said that either one cuts spending on the plan or the public sector generates the resources expected of it, if deficit financing is to be contained.

Since improvement in the performance of the public sector is a long term proposition, any immediate reduction of the budgetary deficit with the assistance of the public sector can come only by the budget being relieved of the duty of providing resources for the public sector. This is already happening with many of the more successful units including the Railways taking increasing recourse to the capital market by the issue of bonds and similar instruments. A logical extension of the idea could be participation in the equity of the successful public sector companies by the general public. The government which is the owner of the shares in these companies could divest some of its holdings to the general public and use the sale proceeds for various purposes including reducing its budgetary deficit.

Britain has been doing precisely this for several years by selling (at a premium) shares of British Telecom and British Gas and the like. We could do same without any of the ideological fervour for privatisation that the Thatcher government has brought to the affair. In a sense, this would make the public truly public and not simply a state sector. It is time that this idea was examined objectively without any ideological hangups.

For the rest, there is scope for the enlargement of the tax base, more determined action in preventing leakages of revenue and tackling the all too visible permeation of black money into the very texture of our economy. Much has been written about this problem and there is little that one could usefully add except to suggest more vigorous administrative action on tested lines. For example, a simple survey of the luxury buildings that have come up in Delhi should establish whether or not they could have been built out of taxed income. The result of this investigation which should not take long--indeed it might already have been carried out by the tax department--should be made public.

On the second problem of getting the better of inflation, no short cuts, except in terms of supply management (which will have its impact on the balance of payments), are possible. The sooner this sinks into public consciousness the better. All solutions, including the containment of budgetary deficit, reducing excess liquidity in the economy (which will have a decelerating impact on growth) and changing the production pattern and income flows to enable the poor to have higher purchasing power, are long and medium term in their reach. The proposed shift in emphasis from the undifferentiated pursuit of growth to a development strategy and production pattern that provide work, incomes and the wage goods that the large majority of the people need would itself generate impulses that will moderate the rigours of inflation on the poor.

The third area of immediate concern is the growing imbalance in external accounts. It is a problem that has been with us in one form or another for decades. But its ramifications have changed over time. It existed even when we had a restrictive import policy. During the eighties themselves, the nature of the problem has changed between the first half and the second. This is partly because the spectrum of imports and exports has undergone dramatic changes and our receipts from "invisibles" and capital account have also undergone drastic alterations in profile.

During the first half of the eighties, exports performed relatively poorly and the value of imports grew, despite a striking reduction in petroleum related imports (and relative stability in their international prices). Other imports, including food related imports like edible oil and capital goods, increased and exports amounted barely to half of the import bill by mid-eighties. On capital account, inflow of remittances from Indian expatriates grew during this period and recourse to the IMF loan facility provided in cushion that the sixth plan needed.

In some contrast, the second half of the eighties saw a remarkable growth in exports in real terms but imports continued to outstrip exports and the nature of capital account movements changed for the worse. Import liberalisation continued as part of the overall policy of "opening up the economy". Indigenous production of petroleum products (whose growth in the earlier quinquennium made possible reduction in imports) reached a plateau, growth in expatriate remittances tapered off and repayment liabilities of IMF and other loans made deep dents on reserves.

A worrisome aspect of the external accounts was that current account deficits were being increasingly financed by short term commercial borrowing, at high market rates of interest. What made these desperate remedies resorted to towards the end of the Rajiv regime even worse was the lack of transparency in these transactions, which were often put through by the overseas branches of Indian banks and similar other agencies as part of their "normal" activities.

These capital account transactions have created fears of an "external debt trap" as an analogue of the internal debt trap. Though nowhere near Latin American proportions, with a debt-GDP ratio of around 60 per cent, India's external debt, including NRI deposits, is around 20 per cent of GDP. It is serious enough to cause worry. This is particularly so since the component of "official debt" is going down and commercial borrowings have increased strikingly in the recent past.

In absolute terms, India's external debt has grown from Rs 18,400 crores (US $ 26, 466 million) at the end of 1980-81 to Rs 68,831 crores (US $ 44,032 million). The figures in dollar terms incidentally reflect the deterioration of the external value of the rupee, another worrying aspect of our external economic predicament. Inclusive of NRI deposits, external indebtedness stood at around Rs 83,000 crores at the end of March 1989 and this figure is expected to go up during the year.

There is little that the new government could do in the short run to reverse these trends. A reduction in domestic fiscal imbalance would go some way in reducing export costs and providing a competitive edge for our products in overseas markets. A reduction in the "import intensity" of exports is inescapable as part of import rationalisation for getting the better of external payments difficulties. On imports for domestic needs, a great deal of sophistication is called for in any attempt at correcting the imbalances that have developed. A mechanistic approach of "across the board" reduction would be counterproductive and the preferred method should be fiscal disincentives to imports rather than physical controls. There is considerable scope for reduction in imports for purposes of price management, especially of "food-related" items of consumption like edible oils by concerted attempts at increasing domestic production. Capital goods exports would offer the toughest, multi-faceted dilemmas and contradictory counsel by opposing interest groups. The "craze for phoren" and the tendency to go in for "package imports" that perpetuate a "screw driver" technological culture is real. But unless domestic production of comparable goods achieves a minimal level of cost and quality attributes, the case for imports, urged by "user industries" cannot be lightly brushed aside. The general thrust, however, should be towards importing intermediates and raw materials rather than the final products. Finally and most importantly, the reordering of the production pattern to conform better to the needs of the poor should itself reduce a good deal of the imports that serve, directly and indirectly, the needs of the relatively affluent.

There is now a recognition that the time is ripe for moving away from a pursuit of undifferentiated economic growth the impact of which on the quality of life of the vast majority of the people of the country has been minimal. The feeling has also grown that there is much that is spurious about the kind of modernisation that has been on the agenda in the recent past. Its most visible manifestation has been the replication of the ambience of the richer countries, with Delhi and Bombay aspiring to be versions of Washington and New York. Amidst the squalor of rural and urban poverty, the vulgarity of the imitative consumerist culture this has given rise to is appalling. Not so long ago, Indian poverty was bearable if only because there was a cultural ambience of austerity and minimal commodity fetishism. All this has visibly changed.

But all this does not mean that we have to revert to a command economy or the perpetration of dysfunctional controls that merely increase bureaucratic power arbitrarily exercised. By definition, decentralisation means dispersal of decision-making in conformity with well understood socio-economic objectives

What are the chances of success of this new strategy of development? Affected vested interests, including the burgeoning middle class (whose size is comparable to whole populations of several developed countries of the West) will feel threatened and use their considerable political and other clout to subvert the new efforts to change course. Competitive politics will create its own tensions and uncertainties.

But the greatest danger is internal. There are many strong personalities within the National Front with strong sectional preferences and opposing ideological prejudices. These might well wreck the short and long-term measures that have necessarily to be adopted both for coping with the immediate crises and for fulfilling the wider objectives for the more distant future. This is apparent in the contradictory formulations in the manifestoes, all of which cannot be pursued at the same time. Some of these, like the write-off of agricultural loans, are already posing a problem to the finance minister who is trying to cope with serious budgetary constraints. There is a clear need for re-examining the commitments made and evolving a hierarchy of urgencies in implementation. Once this is evolved, individual members of the government and the party should observe the minimal discipline of not talking out of turn and committing the government to positions it may not be able to redeem.

# 3

## *The Challenge of Kashmir*

**Balraj Puri**

The agenda of the National Front government, as announced by the prime minister in his first policy statement accorded high, priority to Kashmir. No doubt, the V.P.Singh government has inherited the problem. But the situation in the sensitive border State sharply deteriorated under the new government, mainly due to two factors. Firstly, the kidnapping of the union home minister's daughter and her release on terms dictated by the terrorists raised their morale to a new height and legitimised kidnapping as a political weapon. It had been earlier disapproved by the Muslim world and had tended to isolate the terrorists from the people of Kashmir.

Secondly, the resignation of chief minister Farooq Abdullah in protest against the appointment of Jagmohan as governor of the State, and the subsequent dissolution of the State Assembly, removed a buffer and a middle ground, however small, between the rebels and the Centre. The sudden crack-down by the paramilitary forces at a late hour in the night for massive search operations in Srinagar, soon after the imposition of the new rule, provoked desperate reaction from the people and brought them to the streets in defiance of curfew, leading to a heavy toll of human life.

Two questions are asked in this connection. First, how could a docile timid and non-martial community take to arms? Second, how could a community favoured with lavish Central aid be so ungrateful? Many Kashimiris find in terrorism an answer to perpetual taunts and ridicule about their character implied in the first question. Gun shots herald their initiation to a martial status and hence provide them with enormous thrill. The second question erroneously assumes that money can be a substitute for the satisfaction of political urges. In reality, it stimulates them. It can also provoke a people if they suspect the motives of the aid-givers. Further, aid becomes counter-productive if the manner in which it is spent causes corruption and economic and political distortions.

In order to understand the behaviour of Kashmiri Muslims it must be remembered that they are Kashmiris as well as Muslims. At the time of partition of the country, they perceived a threat to their Kashmiri identity from Pakistan which refused to concede their right to decide their fate. At first, it recognised the right of the ruler to do so and later assumed it for itself and tried to enforce it through a tribal raid. A self-respecting community like the Kashmiris could not accept that position and, therefore sought Indian armed help to defend their right of self-determination.

Thus the threat from Pakistan to Kashmiri self-respect and identity on the one hand and Gandhi's high idealism and Nehru's appreciation of Kashmiri aspirations on the other provided the moral, emotional and ideological basis of Kashmir's association with the rest of India. There were, however, divergent perceptions in Srinagar and Delhi of the fateful decision of the Kashmiris to accede to the Indian union. The rest of the nation regarded it just another instance of the process of integration of the princely states. But for Kashmiri Muslims it was an enabling provision to seek help from a powerful neighbour to protect their identity from the aggressor. The eulogistic references to what was called Indo-Kashmir *friendship* by Kashmiri leadership in that period underlined the separateness of Kashmiri identity. It, therefore, exercised its legal right, under the Independence Act and the Instrument of Accession, to retain its autonomy within the Indian union which other princely states, under their own compulsions, had agreed to surrender to the Centre.

The Kashmiri leaders grudgingly conceded, under the persuasion of the Central leaders, to cede more subjects to the Centre but resisted further pressures to conform to the uniform pattern of Centre-State relations in the country. Article 370 of the Indian Constitution and the Delhi Agreement between Prime Minister Jawaharlal Nehru and Kashmiri leader Sheikh Abdullah in July 1952 eventually formalised the State's constitutional relations with the Centre.

On a representation made by the present writer, Prime Minister Nehru agreed to extend the logic of Article 370 to state - region relations to allay the apprehensions of Jammu and Ladakh. In a joint statement on 24 July 1952 Nehru and Abdullah declared that the constitution of the State would provide for regional autonomy. This arrangement might have provided a stable basis for reconciling regional urges within the State and its status within the country. But this agreement was not acceptable to the Bharatiya Jana Sangh which along with the Jammu Praja Parishad launched an agitation for abrogation of Article 370. More than anything else it shook the faith of Kashmiri Muslims about the security of their identity within India. A number of other factors also contributed to the first emotional rupture between Kashmiri nationalism and Indian nationalism marked by Sheikh Abdullah's dismissal from power and detention in August 1953.

By that time, the Muslim aspect of Kashmiri identity, too, had asserted itself. But as there was a leader like Sheikh Abdullah to articulate and symbolise the alienation of the Kashmiri Muslims, their ideological umbilical cord with the rest of the nation was not cut. And it was possible to win them back in 1975 for a settlement within the Indian union with a renewed assurance that Article 370 would be kept intact, though they remained bitter over the erosion in content of the Article during the period of Abdullah's wilderness.

The unitary constitution that the constituent assembly of the State adopted in 1956 had a built-in provision for overcoming inter-regional tensions. For, nothing threatens the unity of a heterogeneous people more than a unitary establishment. Taking note of my campaign for constitutional, institutional and political measures for inter-regional harmony, *The Times* London observed:

"Mr. Puri argues with justice that until Jammu and Kashmir draw closer, settle their differences, and agree to operate as equal partners, there will never be a stable basis upon which relations with (the rest of) India can be satisfactorily settled."

The mediatory role that I played between Sheikh Abdullah and national leaders like Nehru, Jayaprakash Narayan and Indira Gandhi from 1953 to 1975 was based on my formula of autonomy for the State within India and autonomy for the regions within the State. What facilitated this role was the common ideological framework of Abdullah and the national leadership. He was returned to power in 1975 following an accord between him and Indira Gandhi under which the latter committed the government of India to permanent continuation of Article 370 though he remained unreconciled to erosion of the autonomy of the State during the period of his wilderness since 1953.

However, Abdullah did not honour his part of the agreement regarding regional autonomy. He was encouraged to do so by the Congress and the Jana Sangh. The State thus continued to be governed by a unitary constitution which continued to generate regional tensions and by implication Centre-State tensions.

Apart from the Indira-Abdullah accord the first fair election of 1977 to the State assembly had a great integrating influence on the Kashmiri mind. It demonstrated the vitality of Indian democracy and made the Kashmiri Muslims realize the full potentialities of Indian citizenship. That the Janata Party which ruled at the Centre could be defeated thrilled them and brought home to them the fact for the first time that loyalty to the Government of India was not a necessary condition for loyalty to India.

The Kashmir policy of India has been based--implicitly and explicitly--on the theory that all secular and what are called pro-India forces should unite under one party to fight communal and anti-India forces. The policy has been supported by the national press and political commentators. Empirical evidence on the other hand conclusively proves that whenever there was a secular opposition party in the State, it provided a nationalist outlet to popular discontent, in the absence of which it was forced to seek a secessionist outlet. The present writer had taken the initiative to form the first opposition party in Kashmir by setting up a unit of the PSP but along with Asoka Mehta and other national leaders was beaten up in the streets of Srinagar by goondas of the ruling party and normal functioning of the party was made impossible. Other attempts at formation of secular opposition parties in the Valley met similar fate.

This lack of outlets for ventilation of discontent is another reason for Kashmiris' alienation. Before the Rajiv-Farooq Accord of 1986, the Congress was the principal channel of discontent against the State government while the National Conference channelised discontent against the Centre. As the two parties formed a coalition government, hailed by political commentators as consolidation of secular forces, both types of discontent were diverted to communal and secessionist outlets. Lack of democratic tradition, civil liberties and free elections further forced popular discontent to seek outlets outside the Indian system.

Farooq Abdullah whose party was duly elected to power in 1983 was dismissed a year later mainly for hobnobbing with the opposition parties in the rest of India. As he was forced to share power with the Congress which as a ruling party at the Centre had dismissed him, his role as an instrument of Kashmiri protest and a symbol of Kashmiri identity was shattered.

In a similar way the Akali Dal's role as an instrument of Sikh protest had been shattered following the Rajiv - Longowal accord. I had, therefore, publicly warned in 1986 that Farooq might go the Barnala way. I would have been the happiest person if my warning had been heeded and used to prove me wrong.

While the National Conference-Congress coalition blocked secular and nationalist outlets of discontent, the assembly elections of 1987 which were widely perceived to be unfair blocked the democratic outlet. Alienation of Kashmiri Muslims is thus the result of a cumulative process. Kashmir was the only State of India which had an option to accede to Pakistan but preferred India. It was constitutionally and politically entitled to retain its autonomy within India but was forced to integrate, mainly under pressure from Jammu which was denied its rightful status within the State against the wishes of its majority.

Again Jammu and Kashmir is the only part of India where regional identities have not been recognised. Its unitary constitution forces the people to align on communal lines. It is also the only State of India where the central government (with the exception of the Janata Government in 1977-79 and the present National Front Government) has always imposed a government of its choice (however, unpopular, repressive, corrupt and inefficient it may be). Where one-party government has been the norm, where support to the Government has been made synonymous with loyalty to the country and where demands for democratic and human rights and protests against corruption and administrative injustices are branded as treason, terrorism naturally thrives. If a deliberate experiment had been launched under controlled and most favourable conditions, with Kashmir as a laboratory, to implement a text book model of terrorism, it could hardly have improved upon the present situation.

Farooq's administration was certainly not able to administer the State properly. But subsequent events have belied the presumption that his maladministration was the sole cause of alienation of the people of Kashmir and that his removal would end it. Terrorism in Kashmir, and for that matter anywhere else, is neither due to administrative excesses and lapses nor to poverty and unemployment as such. As a political phenomenon, it is unrelated to individual grievances. It is able to articulate discontent of a community--religious or ethnic--when it suffers from a sense of discrimination and deprivation--more in terms of political power than economic benefits–and comes to believe that its dignity and identity are threatened.

Community discontent, again, is a necessary but not a sufficient condition for the rise of terrorism. It draws sustenance from and shelter in a community that is alienated from the system which fails to provide non-terrorist channels of protest. In the case of Kashmir, a secure source of supply of arms and training facilities across the border made the task of the terrorists easier. It is beyond the capacity of any particular government in the State to provide all these ingredients of terrorism. Its genesis must be traced to the wounded psyche of the people and the system in which they are placed.

To say that Muslims are after all Muslims and could not have behaved differently would not provide an adequate clue to the present phenomenon. For these very Muslims behaved differently in 1947 when they overwhelmingly and of their own accord opted for India. They had then perceived a threat to their Kashmiri identity from their co-religionist Pakistan.

Kashmir poses the gravest challenge not only to the stability of VP Singh's government but also in a much wider sense to the whole country, its integrity, stability, polity, secular democracy, federalism and moral values. Similarly, terrorism threatens the Kashmiri tradition of free thinking and tolerance--without which no civilised society can grow--more ruthlessly than any authoritarian regime could ever do. It would brutalise one of the most humane and cultured communities of the sub-continent and jeopardise its 5000 years old rich heritage.

Kashmiris might have to learn better ways of articulation of their urges and better techniques of protest. But they deserve not condemnation but empathy and understanding from the rest of the nation. People outside Kashmir often resent what they consider special treatment for the State and its appeasement by the Centre. Appeasement certainly does not win friends. But in what respect is the state differently treated from others? Financial aid?

As pointed out earlier, the pattern of Central aid to the State made it counter-productive.

It was the vacuum created by the collapse of politics through normal means -- party system, elections, civil liberties -- that terrorism which is politics through other means, sought to fill.

The Indian State is no doubt powerful enough to meet the challenge of Kashmiri secessionists and also to strike a crushing blow at Pakistan if it embarks upon another armed intervention in their support. But would the moral and political health of the nation remain intact if a part of it remains alienated, humiliated and subjugated? Is it beyond the ideological and intellectual resources of the country to accommodate the legitimate aspirations of Kashmiri people? Why is the grand coalition of the Kashmiri nationalism, Muslim fundamentalism, urge for self-government and fight against discrimination being encouraged to consolidate itself and forced to seek a secessionist outlet ? What is being done to contain the Hindu and Buddhist backlash in Jammu and Ladakh respectively and prevent the Muslims of the two regions from being pushed into the Kashmiri Muslim uprising? Are the administrative and political forces of the State strong enough to prevent a possible vicious communal chain reaction?

The challenge of Kashmir raises a few broader issues also. Would a chauvinistic brand of nationalism be able to ensure national unity and a free society? Can the might of the Indian State be maintained without moral and ideological strength, emotional cohesion, wisdom, vision, and compassion?

# 4

## *Secular Ethos and Minorities*

George Mathew

In a plural society like ours, conflicts of interest based on religious differences are natural. This land gave birth to great religions and also extended refuge and hospitality to the followers of other religions from various parts of the world over the centuries. The resultant social situation poses a challenge to us, the people of India, to create a society where every citizen, irrespective of his or her religion, can live in equal dignity and security. This is easier said than done because of conflict of interests, tendency of party politics to impinge on social problems and complexity of the emerging social forces.

The coming to power of the National Front at the Centre replacing a long spell of government control by the Congress party with its different suffixes is a watershed at the dawn of the 1990s for majority-minority relationship in the country. In this context, the following questions are pertinent. Why did the Congress (I) lose the confidence of the minorities? What are the issues at stake ? What clinched the Muslim votes for the National Front ? What is the emerging scenario under the National Front Government ? What will ensure the confidence of the minority communities in the system ?

The rapid decline of the Congress party's ability to protect the delicate balance in the majority-minority relationship was one of the reasons for its rejection in favour of the National Front at the hustings. In other words, the secular credentials of the ruling party have eroded and touched the lowest ebb. This paved the way for the minority issue becoming a central subject for debate in the elections. A brief look at the two principal minority communities, *viz.*, Muslims and Christians, and their growing alienation from the Congress(I) is important to understand the challenges before the National Front government on the minority question.

The Muslim perception of the Congress (I) was that the party's interest in the community was as a vote bank. Therefore, vocal sections of Muslims began to see through the game played by the party on Muslims. The Congress rule in State after State showed the negative policy of the party. Except the Kanyakumari Hindu-Christian riots of 1982, in almost all the other communal disturbances--and they are legion--the main victims are Muslims.

According to the union home ministry figures, on an average 26.58 communal riots took place in India every month. During the Janata period of 1977-79 the incidence came down to 14.8 a month. From 1980-84, it went up to 34.37 cases a month. From 1985, during the Rajiv rule, it crossed the 45 mark per month. (In 1988 alone there were 611 communal riots.)

Although the police charge-sheeted the accused in the resultant criminal cases nothing happened after that. Almost 99% of them were withdrawn by the governments which did not want to see the culprits punished for fear of losing their votes. There were only two major exceptions--one at Rourkela in 1964 and some cases at Bihar Shareef in 1981.

The guilty have been identified in many of the reports of the commissions of enquiry like Justice Jagmohan Reddy's report on the Ahmedabad outrage of 1969; Justice Madon's report on Bhiwani 1970; Justice Mathew's report on a Kerala incident of 1971; Justice Saxena's report on Moradabad 1980 (Idd day, Iddgah police firing); Justice Narayan's report on Jamshedpur, 1979; Comptroller and Auditor-General of India's report on the genocide of Muslims of Hashimpura and Maliana by the police (which has been supported in 1987 by the report of the Amnesty International and a large number of non-Muslim journalists, as published in *Sunday, Ravivar, India Today, Indian Post* (Bombay) and *The Telegraph* (Calcutta) to mention only a few) and Justice Mishra's woclly-woolly sort of report on the anti-Sikh pogrom in Delhi in which 3,000 persons were killed in three days (1 to 3 November 1984). But not a single person has so far been arrested in the resultant cases. The Congress(I)'s role in fomenting communal tensions and provoking riots in the expectation that the resultant sense of insecurity will make them vote for the party is no secret today. Communal riots were endemic in the Congress (I)-ruled States. The Congress (I) has manipulated and created the great divide between Hindus and Sikhs and Hindus and Muslims.

Further, the Muslims had other complaints too. They know that their share in the services which was 25% to 30% before Independence has plummeted 1% to 3% in Central or State services. No Muslim has been taken into the Central Intelligence Bureau (not Central Bureau of Investigation), the RAW and the special branches of the State police in the Congress governments.

Before the police action in Hyderabad there was a full-fledged Osmania University, where the medium of instruction was Urdu and even medicine and engineering were taught through that medium. But the Congress government dismembered the university while claiming to encourage the growth of Urdu. Thus, the Muslims have come to realise that the Congress has deceived them with platitudes and double standards. They even began to feel that life and honour of the Muslims were not safe under a Congress regime. It had until recently the cake and had been eating it, too, using the misery of the people cynically for electoral advantage.

The Christians, who constitute 2.6% of India's population, are not a militant minority. They have been staunch followers of the Congress considering the Nehru family as their saviours. But the hollowness of this position is slowly being realised by certain sections of the community. It was a Congress government in Madhya Pradesh which in 1954 appointed the Bhawani Shankar Niyogi Committee to enquire into the activities of the Christian missionaries. The committee's report in 1956 was an anti-Christian report, intolerant and sectarian. This was just the beginning. In 1962 the minorities' rights protection committee of the All Kerala Catholic Leaders Conference, feeling betrayed by the Congress, said in despair :

> The Christian community has been solidly behind the Congress, and this distinction cannot be shared by any other community in this State. But, unfortunately, our role seems to be quite peculiar. We are expected to vote Congress and then keep quiet! We are expected to bear the brunt of election expenses; but the self-same politicians, who enter the legislatures with our votes and money, deliberately harm us, once they are in power by raising the communist bogey ! Although our community's contribution to the economic and educational advancement of Kerala has been disproportionately larger than our numerical strength, we have been noting with regret that a concerted attempt is being made to drive us to the wall in all possible ways.

Again it was the Congress governments of Orissa and Madhya Pradesh which passed acts in 1968-69 imposing arbitrary restrictions on the religious activities of Christians. This was followed by Arunachal Pradesh. The Congress government's attempt in the early seventies to interfere in the consecration of bishops saying that the Church should clear the names of the candidates from the government at the pre-notification stage has not been forgotten. They feel that there is vicious discrimination against minority Christian educational and medical institutions in the Congress(I)-ruled States.

Expulsion of Christian missionaries who have been doing excellent work for decades with the local people, accepting Indian ways of life, on the basis of complaints by local Congress leaders were not rare. Christian organisations are indulging in anti-national activities and their patriotism is suspect.

At a general level even the Christian followers of the party believe that the Congress(I) plays the Hindu card for votes. In 1977 the Congress resorted to propaganda that the Janata candidate in Muzzafarpur was a Christian and therefore the Hindus should not vote for him *(Indian Express*, April 4, 1977).

A sizeable section among the Christians now realised that minority rights are best secured not exclusively as the rights of a particular section but as democratic rights of *all* citizens. They concede that a policy of indifference to general well being and the rights of others in the name of minority rights is self-defeating. It was in this spirit that Christian leaders like Raja Maharaj Singh, Prof. M. Ratnaswamy, Dr. H.C. Mukerji and Father Jerome De Souza gave up communal representation for Christians in the legislatures and other special safeguards. Their conviction was that the best safeguards of a religious community were the fundamental rights of all the citizens guaranteed by a democratic state. Such a thinking is getting strengthened among the Christians today. This school of thought represented by Catholic, Protestant and other Christian clergy and intellectuals, has questioned the approach of the church that if one is a Christian she/he should vote for the Congress(I).

In this context, it is important to look at the brief non-Congress interregnum at the Centre to appreciate fully the National Front's position, for the present is in more than one way a continuation of 1977-79.

The Janata Party came to power on the crest of the mighty democratic wave of 1977. By then the Muslim community had been feeling thoroughly disillusioned with the Congress. In 1977 for the first time the Muslim community broke away from its dependence on one leader and one family. They voted for restoration of democracy. Their faith reposed in the new party was not in vain. The Janata government took strong steps to curb communal violence. The then prime minister Morarji Desai had directed the State governments to see that the minorities were represented in all law-enforcement agencies, the intelligence network was tightened to prevent outbreaks of violence, the guilty in cases involving communal violence were speedily brought to book and those who suffered loss of life and property were fully compensated.

During the two years--1977 and 1978--the average number of communal incidents in the country was much less than that during the earlier ten years of Indira Gandhi's rule. The loss of life was certainly much less.

The great achievement of the Janata government was the establishment of the Minorities Commission at the Centre with a clear charter to look into the persistent grievances of the minorities and to suggest ways and means of implementing constitutional safeguards for them. Unfortunately, the government could not pass the bill making it a statutory body before the Lok Sabha was dissolved.

The National Front has got the Janata legacy and ideology and a majority of its leadership belongs to the Janata tradition. Therefore, the present government has a clear headed and sincere policy towards the minorities.

The National Front manifesto is categorical that the religious minorities will enjoy the fullest protection and opportunity to pursue their modes of worship and religious beliefs and practices and develop their institutions, whether religious, cultural, educational or welfare oriented. "Complete non-interference will be observed in their personal laws, their cultural advancement and fulfilment of their distinctive cultural identities," says the manifesto.

Taking the tragic occurrence of communal riots seriously the National Front has committed itself to putting down violence, by effective prohibition of incitement of communal passions and by pursuing appropriate recruitment policies in the police services. It has proposed creation of a mixed anti-riot force to ensure impartial conduct from them. The Front has assured the people that if a riot occurs the victims will be fully compensated and action taken against officers failing in their duty. Special courts are promised to be set up to try cases relating to communal and caste riots. It has started taking steps to punish the guilty of the 1984 anti-Sikh riots in Delhi and elsewhere.

Besides giving the Minority Commission statutory status, in order to remove unemployment and economic backwardness among the minorities the National Front, according to its manifesto, would initiate the following steps :

1. Setting up Minorities Financial Corporations.
2. Representation for minorities on various recruitment committees and boards.
3. Encouragement for establishment of technical and polytechnic institutions by minorities.
4. Preservation of the minority character of the educational institutions guaranteed under the Constitution.

Generally, manifestoes have little influence on the outcome of elections. But during the 1989 elections the National Front manifesto was keenly studied and discussed to understand where the new political formation stands. Besides the manifesto, several other events made the Muslims believe that they can depend on the National Front. At the same time, they exposed the anti-minority character of the Congress(I).

The permission granted by a Congress government to the Vishwa Hindu Parishad (VHP) for the ceremonial laying of the foundation (shilanyas) for a Rs. 55 crore granite temple on disputed land in Ayodhya on November 9 agitated the Muslims. They feared that the temple, when created, would encroach upon the land of the Babri Masjid and bring about its demolition. The crisis became acute when the authorities admitted that the land where the proposed temple was to come up was *nazul* (government acquired) land. They were apprehensive that the issue would be settled in favour of the Hindus with the Congress(I) blessings and that the foundation for a veritable Hindu rashtra would be laid in Ayodhya. The Muslim masses believed that the

Babri Masjid-Ram Janambhoomi controversy was a creation of the Congress(I) government for electoral purposes.

Vishwanath Pratap Singh's resolve to go to Ayodhya on the shilanyas day had a salutary effect on the Muslim morale. Commenting on the move the *Times of India* wrote editorially :

> In a move remarkable for its courage and wisdom Mr. V.P. Singh has reiterated his resolve to visit Ayodhya on November 9 to prevail on the Vishwa Hindu Parishad to abandon, at least temporarily, its plan to lay the foundation stone of a Ram temple at the disputed Ram Janambhoomi-Babri Masjid site. Mr. Singh's forthright stand, which contrasts singularly with the cat-and-mouse games played by the ruling party throughout this volatile controversy, will embolden all those who wish to make it clear to the VHP that its obduracy threatens to place the very existence of India as a multi-religious nation in jeopardy.

The net result was nationwide support by Muslim religious leaders for the Janata Dal.

The communal incidents on the eve of the November poll in Bhagalpur, Sitamarhi, Darbhanga (Bihar), Badaun (Uttar Pradesh), Ratlam, Indore, Mhow (Madhya Pradesh) and Kota (Rajasthan) were largely attributed to the handiwork of Congress(I). Most of these places till now had no history of religious strife. Between January and September 1989, according to conservative estimates, 340 people died in these conflicts. In the November Bihar riots alone more than 200 lives were lost. Naturally, the brunt of it all was borne by the Muslims. The Bhagalpur incidents destroyed whatever faith the Muslims had in the Congress(I) and they shifted in a big way to the Janata Dal and the Left parties. The statement of a Congress(I) legislator summed up the Congress predicament : "We have lost more than what we had gained due to Urdu being made the second language. The problem is that we do not have the face to convince the Muslims that only the Congress can protect them. As a Muslim candidate, I shall still get votes for myself but I'll not be accepted if I try to garner votes for the party."

The Congress had pinned its hopes on the Janata Dal's alliance with the BJP to swing the minority votes towards it. In the case of the Christians it worked but not with the Muslims. The overwhelming Christian support to the Congress(I) was reflected in the election results in Kerala, Goa and the North-Eastern states. But the Muslims sensed the mood of the nation and were not unduly perturbed by the BJP. In fact, they had no reservations regarding seat adjustments between Janata Dal and the BJP as indicated by the following statement of a Muslim leader of U.P. recorded in the newsmagazine, *Sunday* :

> Our experience is that whenever and wherever the BJP (or earlier Jana Sangh) was in power communal riots did not take place. Atal Bihari Vajpayee, who as Jana Sangh leader, used to spit venom against the Muslims and Pakistan, was the *one* who as External Affairs Minister in the Morarji Desai government gave us maximum facilities regarding passport and visas to Pakistan and the Gulf countries. It is because of him that so many Muslims go to the Gulf and earn money as he simplified procedures for issuing passports. In view of all this, why should the Muslims be unnecessarily wary of the BJP?

As electioneering progressed, V.P. Singh was keen on consolidating the favourable response he had from the Muslims. He refused to share the platform with the BJP and that, too, improved his image among the minorities. Today V.P. Singh stands head and shoulder above leaders of other parties in his secular credentials. Like Indira Gandhi and Rajiv Gandhi he is neither going after god men, priests and bishops nor visiting temples and mosques and churches to hoodwink the people.

The National Front has more leaders with proven secular outlook and wholesome credentials than the Congress (I). These leaders who have been supporting civil liberties, human rights and trade union movements are brilliant minds and can make a valuable contribution in safeguarding the interests of the minorities.

At the same time, we must guard against minority communalism for, it breeds virulent reaction in the majority community. If a party tries to appease each community as a community, the rule of law gives way to rank communalism where no one will feel safe. The Congress (I)'s overt and covert communal games in Punjab, Bihar and other places are pointers to this truth. The minority communities have to realise that the protection they are entitled to as a minority is not charity dispensed by any political party. It is part of the constitutional commitment of the entire people to uphold the secular character of India. The track record of the non-Congress parties in the last several years in this regard is better than that of the Congress (I) that has debased this historic social contract with the minorities into an instrument of political deceit.

The crucial aspect of the matter is that the minorities cannot feel safe unless genuine secularism grows in our society. Towards this end a secular stream in all walks of life has to grow as it is. Whenever and wherever communal madnass is unleashed it is this secular stream represented by human rights and civil liberties activists, social action groups, Gandhians, intellectuals, professionals, writers, artists, humanists and politicians strives for sobriety.

Kerala and West Bengal are the two States which can claim to have secular parties and Leftists at the helm of affairs for a long period of time. It is significant that these two States had no communal riots except the planned killing of Muslims by Congressmen in Berhampur in 1988 to malign the West Bengal CPM government.

I am of the opinion that secularism touches upon the condition of consciousness of the masses while fundamentalism does the opposite, the unconsciousness of the masses. How best the former could be promoted should be the concern of us all.

If political power in a democrary pampers a community on the basis of its religion then democrary itself will be endangered. As a sociological fact, human religious identities cannot be erased. With modern communication and mobility the identities will survive, if not get strenghened. Can a leopard change its spots or a scythian its colour? If this is true, then uniformity or a melting pot theory is irrelevant and out of place in the emerging situation. On the contrary, people are becoming more and more conscious of their identity. Secularism is peaceful co-existence of diverse entities. This is a new meaning. The State and the political leadership have a special responsibility to distance themselves from religious expression of the various communities. If State power plays with anything that touches the sentiments of the people--religion is such a social phenomenon--then it plays with fire.

So separation of the State and functionaries of the State from religion is a necessary condition for the development of a secular society in India.

The National Front and its leadership must carefully nurture this aspect so that a civil culture will evolve in our plural situation. Only the emergence of a secular society and a civil culture can eradicate the fear of the minorities about majority intolerance. This is a sensitive balancing act which needs political acumen and vision. That the VHP has postponed the move to construct the Ayodhya temple in response to a request by V.P. Singh and that the BJP is not pressing for the abrogation of Article 370 of the Constitution conferring a special status on Jammu and Kashmir are positive signs for an era of peaceful co-existense of the majority and the minorities under the new political dispensation. These are encouraging signs for the minorities. How they could be utilised for widening the existing secular base will determine the 'Hindutva' resurgence in the country. That it cannot go too far is proved in Maharashtra where even with the BJP the Shiv Sena did not succeed in wresting the state power. The BJP's impressive performance in the Assembly elections can be attributed mainly to its robbing the 'Hindu card' from the Congress(I). The Congress (I) failed to play the game as successfully as Indira Gandhi did; while the BJP succeeded. It is not unlikely that at a later date the Congress (I) may take away the Hindu votes from the BJP.

Prime minister V.P. Singh, his wife Sita Kumari Devi, and West Bengal Chief Minister Jyoti Basu in the presence of Mother Teresa.

V.P. Singh entering South Block, where the office of Prime Minister is located, for the first time in his capacity as the prime minister of India.

President R. Venkataraman with prime minister V.P. Singh and his cabinet colleagues after being sworn in at Rashtrapati Bhawan.

Prime minister V.P. Singh, deputy prime minister Devi Lal, and leader of the opposition Rajiv Gandhi at all-party meet on Kashmir.

V.P. Singh in striking poses as he addresses his first press conference after assuming office of prime minister.

Janata Dal president V.P. Singh talking to media. Also seen (left to right) are Arun Nehru, Jaipal Reddy and P. Upendra

As leader of the National Front V.P. Singh, accompanied by Telugu Desam leader N.T. Rama Rao, calls on President R. Venkataraman.

The prime minister, with deputy prime minister Devi Lal, home minister Mufti Mohammed Sayeed and external affairs minister Inder Kumar Gujral at the golden temple in Amritsar.

# 5

## *A Transitional Phase*

**Devdutt**

With the assembly elections in nine States in the last week of February 1990, the National Front government at the Centre has completed the second phase of the process leading towards self-confidence, stability and self-reliance. The first phase was the one which ended with the vote of confidence in Parliament in December 1989. Therefore, it is time to reflect on the basic programmes and policies of the National Front government in the light of its election mandate which, seen in a perspective, partakes of the nature of a directive to the National Front leadership to go in for an Indian variant of (1) perestroika in regard to the political system, especially the party system, and economic structure; (2) glasnost as well as perestroika in regard to the working of other democratic institutions.

Let us first take changes in the party system. It seems the Indian voter has again made history of a sort. During the past three months he has exercised the right to vote twice in a manner that cracks have appeared in the power structure obtaining in the Hindi belt; he has inaugurated at the Centre the experiment of a coalition government under some sort of collective or group leadership; he has closed the chapter of the unchallenged supremacy of Nehru dynasty in Indian politics. In addition to these changes, the voter has given fresh political directives to bring about basic changes in the Indian polity in accordance with the Indian Constitution. At the fag end of the multi-crore enterprise called Nehru centenary celebrations, the Indian voter announced his decision to restructure in many respects the model built up by Jawaharlal Nehru.

The Hindi belt power structure has been performing the function of the spine of the national movement as well as modern India's democratic structure at the Centre. The region sends 226 members out of a total of 542 to the Lok Sabha. Except for one, all the prime ministers so far have been from this region. The Hindi belt's political elite and leadership set the tone and tenor of Indian nationalism; the political culture of the region determined the character of the Indian National Congress and its leadership. The preponderant influence of the articulate social and economic forces in the Indo-Gangetic plains rendered the Indian national movement as well as nationalism unfinished and incomplete--politically, territorially, psychologically, socially and ethnically. Vast areas situated on the margins of the sub-continent and the margins of the social structure in India remained outside its ambit; even in those areas where the movement was effective, the impact was uneven.

The electoral verdicts of November 1989 and February 1990 have changed the political landscape of the Hindi belt. In addition to the Congress, there are other claimants for supremacy, namely, the BJP and the Janata Dal. In November 1989 the voter has voted out of power the single party Congress government having more than two-thirds majority in eighth Lok Sabha at the Centre and what V.P. Singh himself calls a "minority government supported by the majority" was installed. The ruling partner Janata Dal, has only 144 MPs in the ninth Lok Sabha. In February 1990, the electorate in Gujarat, Bihar, Rajasthan, Pondicherry and even in Maharashtra did not give a comfortable majority to any of the major pan-Indian political parties. In Bihar the ruling Janata Dal is the single largest party but without even 40% of the total seats; in Rajasthan the ruling BJP has 42% of the total of 200 seats. In Pondicherry the DMK and the Janata Dal share power because none has a majority.

Even in Maharashtra the ruling Congress has only 144 out of 288 seats. Not only that, even the State level national parties face challenges from sub-regional parties in some States, for example, the Jharkhand Mukti Morcha contested 26 seats in Orissa, it won 18 seats in Bihar. The Indian People's Front in Bihar won 6 seats and in Rajasthan the United Akali Dal; (Mann) set up candidates in 12 Assembly constituencies.

The new arrangement at the Centre, unlike that which recently emerged in the Hindi belt States, has some unusual and odd features. The National Front government is a strange coalition. A ruling coalition is supported by two non-ruling political parties– BJP and CPI (M) - in the Lok Sabha. Thus we have a sort of a triangular coalition of National Front, BJP and CPI (M). Without the parliamentary support of the non-governing partners the coalition in power cannot survive. This arrangement has been compared to a car, the brakes of which are located somewhere outside it. Obviously it is an odd and risky arrangement. But it appears that the voter was so sick of the menace of continued hegemony of the so-called pan-Indian parties that he did not mind taking a risk with the present type of odd coalition which is a political variant of "living together" or a matrimonial alliance without responsibility.

Further, the coalition is a peculiar mix of poltical forces and parties. Take some major partners. The Janata Dal is a premature child. It was born a few months prior to the general election, marked by a tortuous process of bargaining and unedifying compromises, which continues to bedevil it and render it faction-ridden.

Further, it has yet to acquire the attributes of a regular pan-Indian political party, though some of its leaders have a pan-Indian appeal. It is a conglomeration of various shades of public opinion representing disparate social and economic forces and a few personality-oriented formations. Its socio-economic composition is one of articulate rural middle-classes among the intermediate castes and other backward classes, a cross-section of minorities in urban and semi-urban areas. Specifically, as Madhu Limaye puts it, "it represents a combination of Jats, Yadavs, Kurmis and above all Rajputs (Thakurs) extending from the border of the south to the border of Bengal." Political culture-wise, it betrays unmistakable symptoms of Congress culture; ideology-wise it has left-of-centre inclinations. The Janata Dal is vulnerable to both internal and external crises. So far what keeps the various constituents together is power. There is also fear of loss of public support and fear of chastisement by the public. Otherwise all the factors that led to the precipitate decline of the Janata Party in 1979 are present in an attenuated form within it.

There is the ten year-old BJP with traditions of thought having their genesis in the communal policy of the now defunct Bharatiya Jana Sangh. It is a cadre-based disciplined political party aspiring to fill, in the long-run, the vacuum caused by the collapse of the Congress system in the country. It suffers from stunted intellectual growth. Though it cannot be called backward looking, it has yet to formulate a comprehensive approach to the management of modern political systems and economy. Its political philosophy is based on integral humanism and liberalism, but the mind of the BJP second rung leadership and the ranks is torn between the Congress variant of secularism, a RSS variant of xenophobia, and lumpenized fundamentalism of the Vishwa Hindu Parishad. All of them have their base in urban and semi-urban mercantile classes and commercial interest groups. Geographically speaking, the party is not fully all-India and its social perspectives are not all-inclusive. Then there is CPI(M). Its power base is permanently confined to two States. It is theoretically Left and Marxian but in practice it is highly pragmatic with secular and pro-people orientation. Its sweep and appeal also are not all-India.

It is clear that only one negative purpose keeps them all together, namely, anti-Congressism and oppostion to the dynastic rule of the Nehru family represented by Rajiv Gandhi. Further, the major partners in the coalitional arrangement at the Centre do not have anything common between themselves except the traditions and memories of keen political competition and ideological antagonism. Even during the election campaign in November 1989 V.P. Singh openly practised political untouchability vis-a-vis the BJP. By common criteria, theory and rationality, the arrangement at the Centre may seem preposterous, unthinkable and unworkable. But it is a functioning contrivance which has been thrown up in a period of "functioning anarchy" and disorganization in Indian politics.

In broad idelogical terms, the emergence of the National Front, particularly the Janata Dal, marks the entry of an additional political formation into the middle of the ideological spectrum where the Congress, though defeated electorally, still maintains a strong presence. Thus two middle-of-the-road political formations are competing for supremacy against each other as well as against the BJP in the Hindi belt in particular and at the Centre in general. This is an unprecedented situation which Nehru, throughout his tenure of prime ministership sought to prevent. In this connection it would not be out of place to state that Nehru shaped the Congress into an effective instrument of gaining support and maintaining its continuous hold on the levers of the Indian polity. His ideological disposition enabled the Congress party not only to capture the Centre but also to entrench itself there almost permanently by not only pushing the other parties of the left and the right to the fringes of the poltical spectrum but also by creating conditions for their polarization or fragmentation, specially of the leftist forces. This led to lack of competitive politics at the Centre. The non-Congress opposition was unable to combine or coalesce to provide an alternative government at the Centre.

Today it is a matter of purely academic interest to ask whether this coalitional arrangement is a freak, whether the voter has taken the decision in a huff or on the spur of the moment, whether it is a well-thought out plan on the part of the voter. What is more relevant is that it is an unavoidable product of political compulsions in general and in the circumstances prevailing in 1987-89 in particular.

Moreover, the emergence of the National Front as an alternative to the Congress(I) which, inter alia, singifies the advent of coalition politics at the Centre is a reflection of the political mind of the Indian voter. The Indian voter from 1967 onwards created coalitions at the State level. But upto 1989 he refrained from trying it out at the Centre. Perhaps this was because of an apprehension that only a unitary party at the centre can ensure security and stability of the country. But in 1989, the voter decided to go beyond the make-shift arrangement tried in 1977-79, the emergency arrangement of 1984 after the assassination of Indira Gandhi, and finally, the hegemonistic arrangement called the "Congress system" of governance which prevailed in the pre-1969 period. The voter perhaps realized that the security of the Indian State does not depend on unitary party rule at the Centre. The voter opted for the experiment of a non-unitary, federal arrangement at the Centre, which means restructuring of the party system.

But this kind of restructuring cannot be denoted by the term "perestroika" as understood in the context of the changes in the Russian system since 1985. Every nation, like an individual, has its peculiar problems and challenges and devises its own ways of facing them. The *nirvana* of collective entities is also a unique enterprise; the experience of one nation is of limited relevance for another.

The twin concepts of glasnost and perestroika have been evolved in the context of Brezhnev's and Stalin's legacy. These concepts reflect the mind of the Russian people who, having assimilated the benign results of Soviet revolution over a period of seven decades, are now trying to deal with some of the malignant concomitants of the revolution as well as the dynamics of the positive forces unleashed by the very success of the revolution within Russia and in the rest of the world especially since 1917 and in the context of the post-industrial situation.

The historical context in India is different. Fragmentation is a fact of political life in our country, particularly the party system. The Indian voter has created the conditons for a coalitional arrangement. The emergence of National Front is a response to these conditons. There is no theory involved here; it is plain sound common sense of the Indian mind which is applied in many walks of life, namely, if one whole is broken, and the broken parts are reassembled another whole is created. Disaggregation and re-aggregation are considered two sides of the same coin. But in Russia, the basic structure is intact and the relationship between the parts, inter alia, is being reviewed.

Glasnost which is openness and discussion within Russia, and perestroika understood as restructuring of the Russian economy have little ideological relevance for India which is already committed to liberal democracy with a bias for federalism and to market economy with a big tilt in favour of the public sector. Within this framework, India will have to find its own ways of dealing effectively with some of the congenital or structural ills of the Indian system as well as the operational shortcomings of economic and social developments since 1947. It has been experienced that the structural ills and shortcomings in the functioning of the Indian polity cannot be dealt with by reformism nor by revolution. It has been seen that in spite of ideal conditions for a revolutionary mass upsurge the available revolutionary panaceas have been of no avail, so far the Indian State has proved too invincible and strong for a nation-wide genuine people's revolt. It has also been seen that reformist panaceas have strenghtened the present system. Thus both the methods, namely infructuous revolutionary upheavals and reformist prescriptions have promoted the status quo. As regards perestroika as it is understood today we have our doubts. The National Front has neither a leader like Gorbachev, nor a a party structure like the CPSU; on the contrary, it is a "partyless" government. For perestroika we need to have a party which can mediate between the people and the State.

In a plural society like India, the spread of democratic consciousness unwinds a two-fold process: dis-aggregation as well as re-aggregation, the former is faster, more persistent and pronounced than the latter; obviously, the quest for democracy, inter alia, is also a quest for definition, a search for identity, which being more emotive in nature often takes the form of explosive ethnicity. Therefore, an over-arching movement generally serves as a unifying force and accelerates the process of weaving diverse elements in a plural society into an organic whole. For example, the national movement in India generated pan-Indian consciousness in which certain elements of ethnic consciousness got either dissolved or were worn out or neutralized. Today the momentum of the national movement has been exhausted. Economic development as such cannot be a movement. There is no other uplifting pan-Indian movement which can neutralize the malevolent aspects of the spread effects of democratic consciousness, and thus reinforce the benevolent re-aggregative tendencies.

There is one more dimension to the situation. Democracy and modern bourgeoisie are co-related. The latter, inter alia, is a pre-requisite of the former. Since 1947 the party system in India has been managed and controlled, by and large, by urban bourgeoisie enjoying mass support. This middle class was created during the British rule and was conditioned by some of the ideological dispositions of the national movement. Since mid-sixties new politico-social forces represented by the scheduled Castes and other backward classes on the political scene have emerged. Since they constitute about 70% of the population they deserve a dominant place in the polity. But these classes have not yet thrown up the right kind of middle class. It is true that economic development has created a nucleus of rural middle classes among the scheduled castes and other backward classes. It is also true that the leaders of the rural middle classes are articulating the demands and aspirations of the new political forces. Yet it is not as homogeneous and pan-Indian in its character and sweep as the traditional urban middle class. In some parts of India where they are assertive there is keen competition between them and traditional middle classes. This is one of the reasons for the fragmentation of the pan-Indian party system which was fostered during the national struggle and was consolidated by Nehru in the fifties. The circumstances are not favourable for the emergence of an alternative pan-Indian party system or for restructuring the present party system on an all-India basis.

Surely, the National Front gvernment cannot generate a pan-Indian movement; it is a creature of electoral politics. Therefore, it has a limited role. If its leadership is imbued with a sense of history (which we regret is not visible) it may be able to prepare the political soil for restructuring the fragmented party system. In other words, it can only help the Indian polity to negotiate the isthmus of time between the present and the future when proper social and political forces will throw up a right type of party system suitable for a plural polity.

## II

The Indian voter expects the government to perform the following tasks: (a) to bring about atmospheric changes, namely, openness and other condition of dignity for the common man and society; (b) to restore respect for values and the tradition of accountability of the government to the people; (c) to repair the grievous damage inflicted by Indira Gandhi and Rajiv Gandhi on the democratic institutions and organizations; (d) to deal with specific economic issues, such as inflation, unemployment and poverty which continue to affect the people. The electoral mandate by its very nature excludes direction on strategies and tactics regarding the policies and objectives. It is left to the leadership.

The National Front Government has diagnosed the ills of Indian polity and has formulated a plan of action to deal with them.

V.P. Singh has said the present system is a joint enterprise of politicians, big businessmen and civil servants. He has also said that democracy and nationalism are compatible.

> The country has paid much more heavily because of dead silence in terms of national interest and in terms of decay of democratic institutions. And I think, we should never cultivate that cult. Let us not put poltical unity on a pedestal under which democracy itself is crushed. Many tombstones of democracy bear the inscription unity.

It has been recognized that violence has become an important component of the political culture of India. V.P. Singh has said, "Violence was not in our political ethos and it is a new development for us and it is being used increasingly in various forms. Even in elections... it has penetrated the electoral process. An integrated view of the matter has been taken."

The National Front is committed to the following ideals and objectives:

> ...not replacement of one set of rulers by another, but an alternative model of governance, based on federalism and decentralization, institutional accountability, economic equity and social justice, human rights, freedom of communication and access to information for all citizens, and a responsive and responsible administration and through all this ensure the dignity of both the individual citizen and the nation.

The election manifesto of the National Front spells out the details of the above-mentioned aims: i) The political tasks cover union-state relations, panchayati raj, independence of judiciary, electoral reforms, civil liberties, protection of minorities rights, right to information. (2) The economic tasks are poverty eradication, right to work, steps to deal with wrong policies of the ruling elite, investment in people, full attention to agriculture which has been neglected and exploited so far, inputs and remunerative prices, crop insurance, water management, industrialization; indebtedness, public sector to be freed from bureaucratization. (3) The social tasks relate to the scheduled tribes and scheduled castes, and women.

A time-bound action plan covering nearly all aspects of these proposals was announced on 1 January 1990 (see Appendix III). There are, to our mind, three approaches to examine the policies and programmes of a political party in power. The first is to examine the aims and objectives theoretically and to find out how they are relevant at a particular point of time and in the long-run. The second is the morphological approach, namely, to examine specific items of the programmes and policy, assuming that the basic structure is sound. The third approach is perspectival, *viz.*, to examine the basic structure, its assumptions, *etc*, believing that the specific ills have their roots in the system.The general objectives and aims of almost all parliamentary political parties, especially the centrists, are more or less identical. The differences in the formulation of objectives and aims of these parties are like the difference between different brands of toothpaste.

Hence an analysis of the aims and objectives is of little practical use. In a the morphological approach, the various items relating to policies and action can be grouped under four main heads: a) rectification; b) restoration; c) rehabilitation; and (d) some sort of restructuring. Take, for instance, openness. It is undeniable there has been an atmospheric change after the advent of the new government. The visible or blatant arrogance, remoteness, high-handedness and discourtesy with which the functionaries of the State treated the common people are no longer there. There is a greater measure of courtesy and responsiveness and accessibility.

Some good gestures have also been made. The President of India has declared that the country will have an open government functioning in full public view to reduce the possibility of wrong doing. The President's address to the joint session of Parliament was telecast live. This, speaking metaphorically, is an indication of the openness of the government in the working of parliamentary institutions. The Official Secrets Act will be suitably amended so that people have increased access to information. Doordarshan and AIR will be given autonomy to ensure free flow of information. The 59th Amendment to the Constitution which seriously jeopardised the citizen's right to life was repealed. The Postal Bill which sought to interfere with the citizen's right to privacy will be withdrawn. Similarly, the amendments to the Commissions of Inquiry Act will be removed.

But the major threat to open society comes from terrorism–social terrorism, State terrorism and terroristic activities against representatives of the State and political opponents. The functioning of Indian democracy during the past five years has been deeply affected by terrorism. It distorted the relation between the leaders and the people, the leaders and the rank and file in the ruling party. There is nothing in the programme and policies of the National Front government which comprehensively deals with terrorism as a political phenomenon.

Moreover, "dignity" and openness are not merely a matter of style, namely, one of improved public relations. It is a function of economic security and elimination of exploitative conditions and opportunities for self-expression. It is true the National Front is committed to provide the right to work. But it presumes that the economy is geared for full employment. Therefore, without restructuring the economy for full employment the right to work will mean little.

There are a few other items, *eg.*, land reforms, reform of the planning commission, which hold promise of some sort of restructuring of the economy. For example, the new Government has decided to give "new directions" to planning and development, which according to the deputy chairman had the following three aspects: First, "to make development once again an agent of social transformation and people's liberation... to be considered as a part of the process of creating a democratic, just and decentralized social order. For this purpose, to restore autonomy to planned development from outside interference, either of government or of vested interests (domestic and global) and at the same time subject to scrutiny from forums of public opinion..." Further, the new industrial policy will be job-oriented and the emphasis will shift away from capital intensive programmes. The Centrally sponsored schemes will be cut down. A critical review of the core sector, such as petrochemicals, steel, power, coal will be taken up. The Industrial Policy Resolution(1956) will be reviewed in view of the mounting unemployment. Finally, a selective approach will be adopted in regard to the concept of mixed economy.

The maximum emphasis seems to have been laid on rectification, relief and rehabilitation. For example, an outlay of at least 50 per cent of the resources in the agricultural and rural sectors of the economy is to be ensured in the annual plan for 1990-91. Special measures under the 15-point programme for minorities are to be formulated in the budget session to ensure adequate implementation of development programmes. Further, a scheme to ensure special courts for expeditious disposal of cases relating to caste and communal riots and atrocities will be finalized by March. To give farmers remunerative prices for their produce, the method of computing support price is being altered so that it takes into account inflation from the date of announcement of the prices to the time of marketing. Labour will be costed on the basis of actual wages paid or minimum wages, whichever is higher, instead of the present system where it is costed on actual wages paid. A scheme for debt relief up to Rs 10,000 to small and marginal farmers, landless cultivators and artisans will be finalized. To curb ostentatious and elitist consumption, several measures are proposed. The export-import procedure will be simplified and loopholes in the rules plugged. An employment guarantee scheme is to be implemented progressively.

In consultation with the chief ministers, a comprehensive constitution amendment bill on panchayati raj is to be prepared and introduced during the budget session. Other major proposals are:

1) A national security council under the chairmanship of the prime minister.
2) A high-level judicial commission for appointment and trasfer of judges. Lok Adalats and the legal aid programme will be strengthened by amending the Legal Services Authorities Act.
3) The ministry of defence will examine the modalities of implementing a "one rank, one pension" scheme for ex-Servicemen.
4) Promotion of workers' participation in the management of industries will be given high priority.
5) The measures for improvement of the urban poor include providing basic services and a scheme of night shelters in major cities for about a lakh people in 1990-91.
6) A comprehensive national housing policy for different categories of people and scavengers are to be rehabilitated in medium and small towns in a time-bound manner in 500 towns annually.
7) A commission on women to ensure due representation of women in all spheres, to check discrimination, enforce rights of the women and redress their grievances.
8) A review of the environment policy and laws, to ensure the twin objectives of safeguarding tribal interests and protecting the environment.

The Lok Pal Bill, 1989, described as a major commitment of the National Front Government to prevent corruption in high places has been introduced. The idea of Lok Pal was mooted by the

Administrative Reforms Commission in 1966. The Lokpal and Lokayukta Bill was consequently tabled four times in the Lok Sabha. If one takes into account the total number of committees and the money spent on them and on their travelling in the last two decades the legislation would appear to be the costliest one. In the latest version of the bill, the jurisdiction has been extended. The Lok Pal would be able to enquire into complaints of corruption against the council of ministers including the prime minister. The prime minister will be competent to decide upon action against his ministerial colleagues on the basis of recommendations from the Lok Pal. In case of the prime minister, the Lok Pal will have jurisdiction to indict him or her but will not have the power of punishment. A common element in all these proposals for rectification is that legal provisions are enough for the purpose.

## III

Notwithstanding the fact that the prime minister has often emphasised the need for change in the system, the above mentioned policies do not inspire confidence that the government can even initiate the processes leading to a change of the system. As matter of fact, the policies are based on the assumption that the existing system, which is essentially Nehruvian, is sound and valid. No wonder, the situation has been described in the party's election manifesto as a "crisis of confidence," a "crisis of character" and "crisis of leadership".

It added: "incalculable harm has been done to almost all institutions of the republic- the presidency, the cabinet system, the PMs office, parliament, the legislative assemblies, the administrative structure, the electoral system, the media and the CAG."

In the first instance, this is an incomplete description of the objective situation in India. It is more complex. The polity suffers from several other ills, for example, the imbalance between various constituents of the polity, viz., the state and society, Centre and the

States, the individual and the system, politics and ethics, religion and politics, party and government, 2) serious distortions in the working of various institutions in an era marked by unabashed centralism, unprincipled populism, and cut-throat competition for power, (3) unrealistic, imitative technological development, (4) anti-people patterns of growth in the economy (5) and rise of new middle classes in the rural areas and the assertiveness of an articulate cross-section of backward classes; Therefore, the term "crisis" used in the manifesto does not fully describe or represent the totality of the situation. The word, "crisis" according to the dictionary means a "point or time for deciding anything, the decisive moment (Chambers) or "time of acute danger or difficulty" (Oxford).

The situation seems to be better explained in terms of political sociology, namely, "disorganisation". Every polity has three main constituents, viz, civil society representing social power, political authority representing political power and a set of the institutional mechanisms that mediate and maintain a dynamic balance between the first two. Only if the means of political intermediation and the channels of communication between civil society and political authority are neutral (in the sense that they permit effective and non-discriminatory transmission and processing of diverse interests rather than selectively privileging some interests at the expense of others) can the procedural forms themselves be considered legitimate and worthy of acceptance. "If the adequacy and fairness of these procedures and mediatory mechanism is questioned or becomes suspect, there is a conflict which if unchecked, in the long run, will erode the binding capacity of the institutional forms (eg., political parties, legislature and elections) that aggregate and shape and communicate the will of social and political collectivities."

As on 15 August 1947, when the Indian people entered the era of independence, the Indian polity had the following characteristics. The civil society was feudal, hierarchical, almost static but it had experienced during the preceeding century the stirrings of a sense of dignity, self-respect and nascent nationalism. The political authority was colonial, bureaucratic and centralized; but it had some elements of liberalism and modernity and a network of organized institutions and procedures (for example, political parties, mass media, social movements, electoral system, majority rule, etc) to mediate between civil society and political authority. The polity was congenitally anti-people, incapable of using the vast natural assets and manpower resources of the country for the welfare of the people. It had built-in inequalities and disparities and was unjust and predatory. It had little sources of self-renewal and self-growth.

The primary objective of the Indian national movement *inter alia* was to change this state of affairs. A model of development during the Nehru era was conceived to achieve an egalitarian, free, just and integrated pro-people polity. It is a package of ideas and approaches. It had two-fold functions, in the first instance, to promote the efficiency of the pre-independence polity and to reform it, and secondly in the long run to transform it. In a sense, this model was to serve both as a means as well as an end. It was based on certain assumptions most of which have been explicitly stated by Nehru himself. Firstly, the interests of the country and the people and the efficiency of the system and the welfare of the people are coterminous. Anything that strengthens the country automatically strengthens the people. A proper system automatically ensures the welfare of the people. Secondly, "mass approach or public approach or public meetings approach or small group approach is more effective to change the thinking of the masses and to produce the correct response to any event." It was believed that the people are capable of resisting wrong values and of governing themselves. And that mass basis of policies creates powerful popular pressure. Thirdly, the Congress party with its mass base will continue to be a suitable instrument to achieve the socialist objectives which are said to be inherent in the Congress policies. Fourthly, gram panchayati samitis and zilla panchayats and the bureaucracy will be jointly able to function dynamically and creatively and the village level workers, the agricultural peasants and the officers will not be passive and immune to change. Fifthly, the idea of planning will set into motion certain positive irreversible forces and that planning, in the mind of the common people, signifies hopefulness because it was believed that the best insurance against any throw back is the hope level of our people.

Finally, it was also assumed that the means of political intermediation and channels of communicatioon will at least remain neutral and at best be pro-people and it will strengthen the modern impulses and weaken the unmodern ones within the civil society and thus reduce the parallax or asymmetry between traditionally received patterns and the new pattern.

The strategy adopted to operationalize the above model had three aspects. Firstly, the strategy of "trickle down" effect is valid for India. That State power should be the driving force for all national development effort. It was assumed that the State alone has the monopoly of knowledge and expertise and resources. Secondly, since economic development and social cultural coefficients are of little significance, technology and transfer of technique and resources of power would suffice. In other words, the industrial sector was assigned a key role to create conditions for the transformation of the rural economy. It was taken for granted that the creation of productive assets will ipso facto eliminate poverty and disparities. Thirdly, some of the components of the constructive programme of Gandhi fit well into the Mahalanobis model and will survive it.

These assumptions have been either found invalid or undermined and eroded by the very forces generated by the working of the model. Take, for instance, the balance between the State and society. During the past forty years the civil society in India has been rendered will-less, diffident and dependent. Its capacity for self-renewal has been reduced considerably. Except for periodic rituals of general election, the social power of the civil society is no longer a major corrective of the political authority. Popular pressures do not determine the policies and working of the political authority. In fact, there has emerged a nation-state which, by its very nature, is no better than a command state. The asymmetry between civil society and political authority has been aggravated. The bureaucracy, both political and administrative, has not strangulated the local grassroot panchayats and other institutions, but these have become instruments of state power and patronage. The local power elite is a carbon copy of the national power elite.

The net result is that the degree of people's participation assumed by Nehru and other leaders has not materialized. On the contrary, the voluntary agencies, including the Gandhian agencies, became dysfunctional. The social initiatives got dried up. The State has become all pervasive.

There is one more point. the mass approach did not generate popular movements. On the contrary, electoral politics has displaced mass politics as nexus has been established between development and electoral politics. That the future of the people of India is bleak and that the Indian society will find itself in a state of disorganization if not decay has been very lucidly described in a research study entitled "Overview" by the Ford Foundation. It has stated:"The prospect of India in 2000 A.D. with the continuation of the present policies will indeed be dismal. Even if a social breakdown has not taken place before that time in 2000 AD India will have a huge poverty-stricken, sullen and anti-social population under an economic system in which massive unemployment, in all its forms, will be prevalent... under a social system that is riven with dissensions and strife."

As for the future of the State. "All this is not inconsistent with India attaining a status of a world power by 2000 AD on the basis of her large population, substantial modern and even sophisticated industrial sector and appropriate defence and international political policies. An elite belonging to the business, industrial, managerial, scientific and administrative class and to defence services may manage to achieve the objective of carving out a place for the country in international affairs while remaining perched precariously on a gigantic power keg to explode at any time."

In other words, in 2000 AD the Indian masses will be weak and poverty-stricken and down-trodden but the Indian State controlled by the elite will be strong enough to attain the status of a "world power".

Similarly, economists have often described the situation as "India is a rich country, but the people are poor". But this situation will be compounded by one more element on the eve of 2000 AD. "The Indian State is powerful but the Indian society and people are weak". In other words, in 2000 AD the gap between the Indian State and Indian masses and society will be widened in respect of their relative strengths. The co-existence of an anaemic society and "sullen people and a powerful State ultimately means death of democracy and freedom and the ascendancy of authoritarianism and totalitarianism and even terrorism. To put it bluntly if the twentieth century opened up new vistas of freedom and dignity for our people, the twentyfirst century will open up vistas of unfreedom and decadence and disorganization for our people under an elite managed authoritarian State. In these circumstances, it would be foolish to talk even of social justice not to speak of socialism.

The economy faces many problems. They reflect structural imbalances in the pattern of growth. Here is an excerpt from the report of the Economic Advisory Council, 1989: The decade of the eighties has been a period of relatively higher growth in the gross domestic product at around 5 per cent per annum, which compares relatively favourably with that recorded by most developing countries. Yet the pattern of growth, in methods of licensing employed, both internal as well as external, have been such that, at the end of decade, it would appear that the strategy of growth pursued, especially over the last five years, needs some crucial modification if growth with self-reliance and equity remains the central focus of government's policy. This is because many contradictions inherent in the system have surfaced very starkly of late and will not go away on their own. In other words, though a higher rate of growth in aggregate output was achieved in the seventh Plan, structural imbalances have affected our country."

Nehru's assumptions regarding the character of the Congress party and the role it was expected to play were knocked out. The Congress party underwent a change after 1947. It ceased to be a party which could mobilize people's initiative. It itself became dependent on the state. It had in effect became a part of the State. The lines of demarcation between the party and government got obliterated. Its orthocentre was in the power structure. Hence, its survival depended upon power.

Nehru's faith in the power sector, namely, bureaucracy, political power elites, and other elites has been belied. He thought that the power elite will act as trustees of the people. He saw them in terms of his self image but the power-sector has become predatory. It is in a state of disorganization, morally socially and psychologically. It has been rendered crimogenic. There is politicisation of crime and criminalization of the power sector represented by legislature, party organization, party system, democratic processes, media, judiciary, culture, etc.

It is not merely a case of corruption or criminalization, if the judges do not dispense with justice properly or the teachers do not teach or police does not protect the citizens. In reality it is disorganisation which flows from diminishing concern for ideological perspectives, de-emphasis on the idealist view of life and the demise of belief in utopia. Ideology and ideals, values and norms and good politics are like protective layers of a healthy polity. When these layers get exhausted, then we arrive at the rock bottom of malevolent potentialities of human nature.

Malignancy or disorganization in the organized political and power sectors is manifesting itself in various forms, viz., degradation of democratic procedures and institutions, growth of State power at the cost of social order, disjunction between moral authority and political authority, rupture in the national consensus, and spread of violent ethnic tensions. These specific problems along with the evolution of the nation-State and problems of security have compounded the larger problems of social change.

Sociologically, the working of the model in a particular type of ethos and historical context has thrown up an unmodern ever-burgeoning middle class which is inordinately irresponsible, unrepentantly predatory and irredeemable, and culturally bankrupt. It is politically lumpen and by virtue of its tendencies crimogenic. The character of this class (which normally has played a historic role in the transformation of Europe from a feudal to a modern polity in 19th and 20th century) will further deteriorate in the next few decades on account of the rapid entry of neo-middle classes from the rural areas, especially the weaker sections.

To sum up, during the past four decades the basic assumptions of the leadership of the Nehru era and the strategies they adopted to bring about radical transformation of the pre-Independence polity have proved invalid. The processes and instruments that were supposed to mediate between social power and political power became partisan in favour of themselves and the vested interests and against the people. The process of implementation of Nehruvian policies generated malevolent forces. At worst, what has come into existence is a capitalist welfare democracy which under the present leadership has slipped into a state of disorganisation, if not decadence.

These are the basic tasks of reconstruction of the Indian polity. As it is constituted and given the character of its leadership and organizational skill, the National Front government should not be expected to tackle these tasks within its life span. However, it can play a limited role (1) in not allowing the polity to step back into a Congress variety of unitary pan-Indian system and (2) to prepare the ground for fundamental changes.

Neither the methods of crisis management nor those of resolution of crises are relevant to the prevailing situation. The real challenge is how to deal with the state of disorganisation, *viz*, how the basic assumptions of a polity as conceieved during the national movement under Gandhi can be re-established, how to ensure that the processes and instruments that mediate between social power and political power are rendered non-partisan and pro-people, how to deal with the structural imbalance in the system.

Parliament, as a legislative body, elected on the basis of a mandate enunciated in an election manifesto, however radical, is not a fit instrument to deal with the state of disorganization which calls for system change; it is the prerogative of a Constituent Assembly, elected on the basis of a blue-print of system change.

The National Front government, given its present character and the leadership and numerical strength in the Lok Sabha cannot undertake this kind of enterprise. However, it can play a limited historical role, *viz.*, to ensure that there is the no relapse into the pre-1990 situation in so far as the party system at the Centre is cencerned; not to be obsessed by the idea of fulfilling election promises at any cost, but to telescope some of the items of the election manifesto (concerned with structural changes) into a large longterm programme aimed a dealing with the state of disorganization.

# 6

## *Security : Hobson's Choice*

**Sreedhar**

Any discussion on security perspectives should be preceded by attempting an answer to the question: Security of what ? Like in any other nation state the concept of security involved the preservation and perpetuation of the core values fundamental to the Indian State: values revolving around democratic norms, secular society, federal polity, moral and ethical values, fundamental human rights and above all national strength and power. These values had shaped the Indian civilisation; and they provide the foundations on which modern India can be built by taking into account the historical socio-economic conditions in the country. Given the pluralist character of the society, socio-economic inequalities and regional disparities at the time of Indian independence, it is only through the adoption and pursuit of these values that internal dissonances could be resolved within reasonable limits. This is why these core values are enshrined in the Constitution; and Indian security perceptions revolve round these core values.

### I

Since the second half of 1980s there is a growing realization among the western strategic community about India emerging as a regional power in the South Asian context. This found reflection in statements made by important officials of successive US administrations. Such an open admission by the US was viewed by the Indian strategic community with a feeling that at long last the global community is acknowledging India's pre-eminence in South Asia.

However, a strange thing seems to have happened since then. When the print media started writing about the emergence of India as a 'regional power' on 'mini super power', there is an all-round denial from the highest political authority in the country to an average intellectual. This trend in the print media started around mid-1989; and denials at regular intervals followed it first by the intelligentsia and then by the prime minister's statement in September 1989, that India has no desire to become a super power.

In any discussion of this nature the foremost point to be noted is peculiarities of the Indian subcontinent. India, with almost the size of a continent is surrounded by small neighbours. While India, immediately after independence, started nation building with definite political institutions, the same cannot be said about others with the exception of Bhutan and Maldives. Lastly, India was fortunate enough to have a galaxy of charismatic leaders during the 1950s and 1960s to nurture the politico-social values enshrined in the Constitution. The same cannot be said about India's neighbours. In addition history and geography gave India a pre-eminent position in the Indian subcontinent; and the Indian economic base is vast and all encompassing compared to its neighbours. In other words, a classic case of big power-small power syndrome operates in the Indian subcontinent.

**Basic indicators of south Asian countries**

| Country | Area sq km | Population mn | GNP mn US $ |
|---|---|---|---|
| Bhutan | 46,500 | 1.3 | N.A. |
| Bangladesh | 143,999 | 101 | 15,000 |
| India | 3,166,829 | 767 | 196,500 |
| Maldives | 289 | 0.19 | NA |
| Nepal | 147,181 | 17 | 2,664 |
| Pakistan | 796,095 | 99 | 37,430 |
| Sri Lanka | 65,609 | 16 | 6,267 |

If one accepts the idea of big power-small power syndrome in South Asia, with all its diversities, many of the irritants that crop up from time to time can be explained. When the big power is demonstratively weak like in 1962, after the Sino-Indian war, small powers try to resolve bilateral disputes through use of force like it happened in 1965 and 1971. If we go by conventional wisdom of force levels and military superiority both 1965 and 1971 wars should not have been fought.

The absence of any major military conflict during the last 17 years in the Indian subcontinent is demonstrative of the fact that India won a decisive victory in the 1971 armed conflict; and periodic power projection since then brought in a certain amount of stability to the region.

## II

The immediate question that arises is how India is projecting its power; and what signals it is conveying to others. According to Ross H. Munro in his article 'Super Power Making' in *Time* (3 April 1989), India's power projection can be understood by five major actions in the 1980s :

- Siachen glacier incident in 1984 vis-a-vis Pakistan
- Sumdorong Chung valley incident in Arunchal Pradesh vis-a-vis China
- Operation Brasstacks
- Sending Indian peace keeping force to Sri Lanka
- India sending its military power to the assistance of President Maumoon Abdul Gayoom in the Maldives.

The second and equally important point Munro makes is that of India's quest for military modernization as reflected in increased defence expenditure during 1984-88; and the weapon acquisition and development programmes.

The first three--Siachen glacier, sumdorong Chung valley incident, and Pakistani response to Indian military exercises, Operation Brasstacks--were obviously efforts by Pakistan and China to take advantage of fragile domestic situation in India. The simmering Punjab problem culminating in operation Blue Star in 1984 to flush out militants in Punjab; followed by the assassination of the Indian prime minister and the swearing in of new government under Rajiv Gandhi all created doubts in the minds of neighbours about New Delhi's capability to respond decisively. Apparently the ruling elite in Pakistan during this period could have easily adopted the same de-escalation measures after the Indian response, before also. For instance, when Pakistan was driven out of Siachen, the then President of Pakistan, Zia ul-Haq declared Siachen as a waste land where even grass did not grow. Similarly, during Operation Brasstacks, the Pakistanis moved two armoured brigades to forward positions in the Punjab sector, resulting in massive Indian response all along the Indo-Pak border and this forced Pakistan to defuse the situation by asking for a meeting at the Foreign Secretary level. The proposal was readily accepted by India. In fact, one wonders, why Pakistan, if it had any misapprehension about the proposed military exercises, has not adopted the approach of bilateral negotiations, before thinking of military response at the first instance itself.

India sending peace keeping force to Sri Lanka in July 1987 is a separate case by itself. Unlike the US in Vietnam and the Soviet Union in Afghanistan, India sent its armed forces to Sri Lanka to protect its territorial integrity, and the duly elected government. India has done so in the past in Sri Lanka in April 1971 to protect the elected government of Sirimavo Bandaranaike in Colombo. Of course there was a token participation from some of the other Commonwealth countries along with India in 1971.

In 1987 Indian troops alone went into Sri Lanka under the Indo-Sri Lankan Treaty of July 1987; and are withdrawing the instant both the contracting parties, India and Sri Lanka, felt that a reasonable amount of neutralisation of Tamil militants demanding *Eelam* was achieved.

Indian assistance to the Maldives has been swift and successful. In fact the speed with which India went to the assistance of Maldivians raised some totally unnecessary apprehensions in some quarters. Surprisingly, no one questioned India's legitimacy in assisting M.A. Gayoom to put down the coup attempt.

From the above analysis one can draw three broad conclusions.

India has not shown any expansionist tendencies as apprehended by the strategic community in the smaller neighbourhood. A detailed examination of the documents pertaining to the period of Indian independence shows that the often cited Sikkim case of 1975 does not stand any scrutiny. More than that, Sikkim's absorption into the mainstream political process of the republic since then shows the futility of this argument.

Secondly, there is consistency in India's policy of assisting its smaller neighbours in moments of national crisis--Burma, Nepal, Sri Lanka, Bangladesh and Maldives. In retrospect one can see a certain amount of continuity in Indian policy.

Lastly, Indian polity which is in transition is trying to provide a stable security environment to the extent possible.

## III

This leads us to the next question why a section of Indian elite is unwilling to accept the pre-eminent position which history and geography have conferred on her. One explanation could be the traditional under- playing of virtues among a section of the elite, a typical characteristic of the subcontinental civilisation. Another explanation could be the usual caution, as in any other society in transition, there are many contradictions still in Indian polity which are yet to be resolved before India can consider itself as a regional power in the strict sense of the term. A third explanation could be that a section of Indian intelligentsia's psyche finds 42 years of independence too short a time in a nation's history, after over 200 years of colonial legacy, to assume the mantle of leadership of the entire subcontinent.

These socio-philosophical interpretations apart, some of the stark facts and figures quoted in this regard need to be noted. Indian economy for a variety of reasons got stuck with the Hindu growth rate of 3.5 to 4.0 per cent since 1950; and even after 35 years of planned development 37-38 per cent of the population live below the poverty line. The 1980s witnessed a debt burden of Rs. 52,000 crores (roughly in US dollar terms 3.5 billion); and if corrective measures are not taken immediately India may fall into the trap of proverbial Latin American economies. The precarious balance of payments position in 1989 further reinforces this argument.

The intelligentsia advancing this argument forget the fact such aberrations have occurred in the Indian economy from time to time. In fact, the Indian republic was not able to feed its population in the mid-1960s; and was totally dependent on PL-480 US food aid to feed its population. The balance of payments was much worse then; and in fact at the insistence of the International Monetary Fund the Indian rupee was devalued to boost exports. More than half the population was living below the poverty line.

When the Indian economy was subjected to such stresses and strains, it bounced back on the food front with the green revolution; 17 years later it could voluntarily surrender IMF loan; and Indian economy withstood global inflation remarkably well. The people living below the poverty line came down from over 50 per cent to less than 40 per cent as per the current estimates. All this indicated that Indian economy has acquired the necessary resilience; and can withstand stresses and strains without any serious dislocations. In fact, according to Jasjit Singh in his paper "Strategic and Security Perspectives of India", during the next 30 years, India's gross national product is expected to equal or exceed that of every European country with the exception of the Soviet Union. In other words, the Indian economy is not in a shambles as it is being made out to be; and the long term perspectives are looking fairly good.

An equally important myth that has been spread by a section of the intelligentsia is that defence expenditure is a strain on the scarce resources. However, as can be seen from the following table, while during the disturbed years India's capacity to finance the plan came down drastically, in the subsequent years it increased substantially. This is in spite of the increased defence expenditure in absolute terms.

During the war years and the initial years of improving defence preparedness, that is after 1962, India's capacity to finance her development plans was at an all time high. After 1971, India's capacity from domestic sources substantially increased. This is *inter alia* due to secured environment that has been provided, and the development process could be continued unhindered. In fact, in the 1980's India could come out of the Hindu growth rate of less than four. In other words, there is no empirical evidence to suggest in the long term Indian economy has suffered seriously by an investment of 3.50 to 4.00 of the GNP on defence.

However, the caution from this section of the Indian intelligentsia about the Indian economy is needed to act as a check on the political leadership which can go wayward.

This takes us to the next question--the resurgence of sub-nationalism in India. Basically, the Punjab and Jammu and Kashmir problems can be characterised as the manifestation of this sub-nationalism; and like in the past, the militants in these provinces started getting support from external powers. In military parlance one can classify them as low intensity conflicts. A section of the Indian intelligentsia feels that a nation besieged with such problems at regular intervals cannot claim itself to have completed the nation building process. In such a situation India cannot rate itself as a reg:onal power.

While there is some grain of truth in this argument, one cannot ignore the fact that India dealt with the Mizo, Naga and Naxalite agitations in the east and Telengana and DMK agitations in the south. In fact, the successful absorption of the communists into the nation's democratic process should be considered unique in the contemporary political history of any nation state in the world. This gives the Indian republic confidence that it can cope with the current Punjab and Jammu & Kashmir problems.

**Financing of the Plan (Rs. Crores)**

| Plan | Total public sector outlay | Domestic sources | % to total | External sources | % to total | Deficit finance | % to total |
|---|---|---|---|---|---|---|---|
| First Plan (1951-56) | 1960 | 1438 | 73.4 | 189 | 9.6 | 333 | 17.0 |
| Second Plan (1956-61) | 4672 | 2669 | 57.1 | 1049 | 22.5 | 954 | 10.4 |
| Third Plan (1961-66) | 8577 | 5021 | 58.5 | 2423 | 28.3 | 1133 | 13.2 |
| Annual Plan (1966-69) | 6756 | 3648 | 54.0 | 2426 | 35.9 | 682 | 10.1 |
| Fourth Plan (1970-74) | 16160 | 12013 | 74.3 | 2087 | 12.9 | 2060 | 12.8 |
| Fifth Plan (1974-79) | 41712 | 32943 | 79.0 | 5209 | 12.5 | 3560 | 8.5 |
| Sixth Plan (1980-85) | 110821 | 86608 | 78.1 | 8529 | 7.7 | 15684 | 14.2 |
| SeventhPlan (1985-90) | 180,000 | 148,000 | 82.2 | 18,000 | 10.0 | 14000 | 7.8 |

## IV

However, the immediate question that arises is as we are entering the decade of 1990s, what would be India's security concerns during the next decade ? For any crystal gazing of this nature one has to depend on the experience of the 1980s.

The developments in the 1980s show three distinct trends. The use and threat of use of force to resolve bilateral disputes became totally irrelevant as the 95 month Iraq-Iran war demonstrated. Even before the Iraq-Iran war demonstrated the futility of armed conflict, South Asia enjoyed relative peace since 1972.

At the same time one witnessed any number of low intensity conflicts (LIC) like the company level fighting in Siachen between India and Pakistan. Interestingly, this LIC was accompanied by bilateral discussion at political and military levels. This in a way ensured localisation of the conflict. At the same time, if we keep the Indo-Pak relations aside, India's relationship with all its neighbours followed the familiar pattern of usual ups and downs. Each nation state tried to acquire a pressure point vis-a-vis India and vice-versa.

The resurgence of sub-nationalism and religious fundamentalism surfaced again. As has been mentioned earlier, militancy in Punjab and Jammu and Kashmir looms large before the decision makers in New Delhi. Though qualitatively these are different from the earlier ones like the Mizo, Naga and DMK agitations, the developments in these states during the past few years do pose some challenges to the security of the Indian republic. The situation is undergoing a qualitative change with Punjab acquiring the unique distinction of being the only state in northern India where elections were held to the ninth Lok Sabha peacefully. (One cannot miss the striking similarity at this point of the Punjab problem with the DMK agitation in the late 1960s). With the change of guard in New Delhi, new political initiatives are being taken and it will take some time before some of these initiatives get translated into policy and implemented.

An equally important thing is the developments in socialist Europe and their likely impact on the Indian economy.

In the emerging new setup the trade preferences that India is enjoying, though mutually beneficial, may disappear. With the Soviet rouble getting into free currency category by mid-1990s, the strain on India's limited foreign exchange reserves is going to be substantial. In addition, the concessional aid from the North is depleting in absolute terms; and the developments in eastern Europe may necessitate further pruning down. In these circumstances, competition for resources from the members of the Organisation for Economic Cooperation and Development is going to be intense both in technology transfers and money.

Lastly, the wave of religious fundamentalism though subsided partially, does pose a threat to India's secular and plural polity.

## V

It is in this background one has to examine the options available to the National Front government. Immediately after assuming office, the National Front government apparently proceeded on two principles to shed the big power image by publicly pronouncing that India's defence expenditure will be cut; and secondly, starting a dialogue with all the neighbours to find a way out for some of the outstanding issues with them. From the fourth week of assuming office, the National Front government leadership realized that the ground realities are totally different to pursue the pronounced policies. In fact, the pronounced policies of the National Front appear to have sent wrong signals to some of the neighbours. In their perception, the National Front government headed by V.P. Singh is a minority government in office, with support from extreme right and left political parties. As such it cannot act decisively in any given crisis because of internal contradictions; and this is the most opportune time to extract maximum concessions from India. The best example of this attitude was first given by the outburst of the Sri Lankan foreign minister during his two visits to Delhi after the National Front government assumed office.

The flaw in the neighbours' perception was that foreign and security policies in India are generally pursued by a broad consensus among various shades of opinion. It must be said to the credit of the National Front leadership, that once they realized that the ground realities are different, they were quick to do introspection and announce corrective measures. For instance, by the seventh week in office, the prime minister announced that defence expenditure will not be cut; and by twelfth week he made a categorical statement that defence expenditure will be increased. Similarly, Colombo has been advised to take action to protect the interests of the north-Eastern Sri Lankan Tamils. So were Nepal and Bangladesh.

However, the first major test to the National Front's foreign and security policies came from Pakistani involvement in Jammu and Kashmir. The Pakistani aid to the secessionist movement in Jammu & Kashmir is getting intensified since the beginning of 1990. The National Front government's response was similar to that of the Congress(I) regime earlier: decisive. In early February 1990, the Government's signals indicated that if Pakistan was not willing to stop interference in India's internal affairs, like in Jammu & Kashmir, India would be forced to go to war with that country. Interestingly one could see a gradual de-escalation in Pakistani support to the secessionist movements from the second week of February 1990, almost repeating the January-February 1987 scenario. This attitude of the National Front government received unanimous support even from the National Front intelligentsia which advocated different policies at the time of elections.

The National Front government was able to act decisively because of the investment made in defence ensured a certain amount of defence preparedness; and the political leadership could respond to the challenges posed to it from its adversaries. In other words, India acquired the needed deterrence capability to check its adversaries, and not to allow a repetition of the 1962-71 syndrome. If India lowers her defence preparedness gradually vis-a-vis her neighbours like in the 1950-61 period, the possibility of the adversaries taking chances is high.

In these circumstances, with a permanent threat from neighbours; and with the addition of low intensity conflicts from within added to it the National Front government has no option but to sustain the level of investment in the years to come--that is around 4 per cent of gross national product, at least in the short run. Since defence preparedness cannot be built overnight, any government in Delhi has to cater to the needs of defence; and only from a position of strength can it pursue the policies of peaceful coexistence.

The Muslims' realisation that the Congress (I) was not really a secular party alienated them from it. The inability of the Congress(I) to take a principled stand on important issues affecting the secular ethos of our society lost the support of the minorities to it. Now the Muslims have reposed their faith in the National Front. The socialist stalwarts in the National Front are an added source of strength to the minorities.

The best guarantee for the minorities is not one party or another. Only the emergence of a truly secular ethos will guarantee the safety and security of all. The minority communities and their enlightened leadership have a great responsibility to contribute to the growth of secular society and promotion of a civil culture in India (as opposed to a religious culture) in cooperation with secular forces in the majority community. The National Front government offers a great opportunity for such a social process.

*Perestroika in India*

# 7

# *India and Her Neighbours*

Pradip Bose and G.S. Bhargava

A spectre is haunting India as it enters the last decade of the twentieth century, the spectre of insecurity. While at the popular level it is compounded by growing incidence of violence in public life, promotion and propagation of individual terrorism for largely political purposes and apprehension of threats to the country's territorial integrity, in the case of the leaders of the former ruling party and their advisers it has been a convenient alibi for leading India towards a militarist posture in its international relations, especially with the small neighbours in the south Asian region. Never before in the last 43 years of Indian independence have the country's relations with its immediate neighbours been so strained as during the last two years of Rajiv Gandhi's prime ministership. Official spokesmen and their apologists came to perceive threats to the country's security even from Nepal, Bangladesh and Sri Lanka, in addition to the perennial Pakistani source. In the case of these countries there is also the alibi of "a power vacuum" if India does not involve itself directly in their domestic and international affairs.[1]

It is no small irony that a country which in the 1950s had effectively wielded the psychological weapon to secure its legitimate national interests and ward off perceived threats even from the big powers, a country which in the heyday of Nehru's leadership set the style for nonalignment and, by abjuring arms deals with the super powers, avoided involvement in cold war dialectics, should in the centenary year of India's first prime minister conduct itself like a veritable rouge elephant, flexing its military muscle, violating the air space of Sri Lanka and threatening to reenact a Cyprus or a Lebanon on the ill-starred island.[2] Either bankruptcy in the diplomatic field is leading to undue recourse to military means which is bad enough or the mind set of the policy makers arrogates to India the divine right to force its weaker neighbours to subserve what are perceived to be its security concerns. There can be no worse affront to Nehru's memory than this. To add insult to the injury, it is sought to be justified on grounds of promoting democracy, *a la* the U.S. in Panama and elsewhere in Latin America, or for safeguarding the interests of persons of Indian origin in those countries. This is a pernicious practice which makes Indian settlers in other countries suspect in the eyes of their other inhabitants.

Before describing the problems of India's relationship with its neighbours, it is necessary to underline a major factor in international relations today. Both gunboat diplomacy and a paternalistic attitude by the powerful States towards the weaker ones will neither work nor will they be tolerated. The big powers which tried to replicate the 19 century tactics in the last quarter of the present century have learnt a bitter lesson as the U.S. in Vietnam and the Soviet Union in Afghanistan, not to mention Beijing's experience in Vietnam and Cambodia. The gross national product of a sizeable number of U.N. members is less than that of a single country like the U.S. or Japan. In South Asia, for instance, all the other countries put together cannot match India's military resources and its flair to augment and modernise them. But they are technically equal within and outside the United Nations. They cannot be ridden over roughshod. The nationalist sentiment is very strong, especially among the countries which had won their freedom in the decolonisation wave of the 1950s and 1960s. Countries whose population is less than that of a district in India have a vote in the General Assembly like India. Although the international system is not multipolar in power terms, it does not allow for the dominance of many by some, however powerful, big or benign. The winds of change sweeping our planet cannot be shackled, especially with the revolution in communication technology and the dwarfing of physical distances.

Therefore, the concept of equality among nations--big and small--is no longer a platitude like declaratory allusions to disarmament, elimination of nuclear weapons and fight against pollution. It is a hard necessity for the conduct of international relations. Any small nation whose sovereign rights are infringed is able to garner enough diplomatic support from elsewhere. There are no more "backyards" of the big or super powers left in the world today. The U.S. might have got away for some time with the theory of "vacuum" in the Indian Ocean to spread its military tentacles there but Indian military intervention in Sri Lanka in the name of pre-empting "external" involvement in the region has backfired, with about 5000 casualties in two years plus enormous economic and opportunity cost.

Secondly, the very preponderance of India in the region--in size, population, resources and potential--casts upon it the responsibility to evolve and maintain equable relations with its neighbours. Both industrially and militarily India is much too powerful for them. India's democratic system, despite its shortcomings, has attraction for peoples like the Nepalese and the Bangladeshis and is, therefore, perceived as a challenge by the unrepresentative regimes in those countries. There is, therefore, multi-faceted sensitivity or even oversensitivity in the capitals of these neighbouring countries regarding India's intentions and capabilities. New Delhi should respond to it realistically and not see it either as potential hostility or an opportunity to live up to their worst apprehensions. Thus, a very crucial psychological factor is involved in India's relations with the smaller neighbours and should be taken into account while formulating India's policies towards them. For this reason, it is not enough for India's policies to be "correct" but they should also be perceived by the leaders of those countries to be so. Towards this end, it is necessary to have the right type of personnel in the South Block and in the capitals of the countries to implement policies and project a correct image of India. Then only there will be mutual goodwill and amicability between India and its neighbours.

Unfortunately, even in Nehru's time some of the Indian diplomats in the neighbouring countries did not project a flattering image of this great country. C.P.N. Singh in Kathmandu was a glaring example. More recently, Mani Dikshit in Colombo and S.K. Singh in Islamabad had not only contributed to adoption of "tough" policies but also pursued them on the ground. The Indian mission in Dhaka during the days of Sheikh Mujibur Rehman had been likened by observers to the Soviet embassy in Warsaw in the 1950s.

The third factor is that India being comparatively a much larger country with a greater resource base, the policy makers in New Delhi should be able to display a sense of generosity positively and avoid being petty minded in dealing with governments and peoples. In the early 1960s when one of us was going to Rawalpindi as a correspondent of an Indian newspaper Jayaprakash Narayan's advice to him was that he should try to share the successes and sorrows of the host country. It should be more so in the case of diplomats, especially when the tour of duty is in a country with so much in common with India. But the official Indian attitude at that time was to look down upon Pakistanis as inferior human beings wallowing in Ayub Khan's "basic democracy." The foregoing does not, of course, mean that legitimate national interests should be compromised by the policy makers and their diplomatic instruments but it is necessary to draw the line between national interest and its distorted projection. In the words of Mikhail Gorbachev, "the only solid foundation for security is the recognition of the intrests of all peoples and countries and of their equality in international affairs .... Ideological differences should not be transferred to the sphere of inter-State relations nor should foreign policy be subordinate to them .."[3]

## Nepal

The Rajiv Gandhi regime had been stalling the renewal or renegotiation of trade and transit treaties with Nepal after they expired on March 23, 1989. For a landlocked country like Nepal, it amounted to being subjected to an economic blockade as a result of which the prices of essential goods like kerosene and petrol had risen sharply causing severe hardship to the people. The Indian government's expectation was that popular discontent would pose a threat to the regime forcing it to acquiesce in Indian demands for a single treaty of trade and transit and cancellation of arms purchases from China. Nepal has been asking for two treaties on the ground that while transit facilities for a landlocked country were of a permanent nature, trade relations needed to be reviewed periodically. In 1978 the Janata Government acceded to the request and two separate treaties were signed. Indira Gandhi who returned to power in 1980 accepted the principle of two treaties in 1983 when they were renewed. But in 1989 the Rajiv Gandhi government decided to revert to the pre-1978 position of a single treaty for reasons which remained unexplained. In the absence of elucidation of the rationale for the Indian government's position there was speculation that plain hubris or bruised ego of the Indian political leadership was the reason for the *volte face*.[4]

The arguments of the apologists of the Indian Establishment are revealing. First, King Birendra who succeeded his father in 1972 "has been carrying forward his father's policy of distancing Nepal from India with added vigour and determination."[5] It is not a crime for rulers of sovereign States, be they elected or dynastic, to assert themselves against their larger neighbours. In fact, it is natural and an attribute of sovereignty. B.P. Koirala who was Nepal's only elected prime minister (who had participated in the Quit India Movement of 1942 and shared India's democratic ethos) had lost no time in reminding Nehru in 1959 that India was not Nepal's security manager. The same is the case with the present young ruler of Bhutan, although Bhutan is a virtual Indian protectorate in many respects. Further, King Birendra may or may not have succeeded in distancing Nepal from India but the Indian government accomplished it to a fair measure in 1989 by imposing what was seen as an economic blockade on the Himalayan kingdom.

The cultural ties binding India and Nepal are deep and ages old. That India calls itself a secular and socialist democracy and Nepal is a Hindu kingdom has not diluted them. The geographical proximity is obvious, although it has not always led to amicable relations. While Pakistan has been virtually wooing Nepal despite the religious diversity between the two nations, India has been more solicitous of conservative, pro-American Muslim kingdoms like Saudi Arabia, Iran of the Shah days and Jordan as well as Islamic dictatorships like Iraq and Syria. Nepal nearer home has been a poor cousin for Indian diplomatists. The mutual interdependence between India and Nepal ecologically and in harnessing the waters of the rivers linking the two countries has been another fact of life. Yet, why did King Mahendra try to "distance" Nepal from India ? Why is his son and present ruler perceived to be following in his father's footsteps ? The reasons are many. First, with the communications revolution of the 1950s and the spread of nationalism in the wake of post-war decolonisation, international relations have undergone a qualitative change. In the circumstances, it is natural that Nepal should assert its independence and be also extremely zealous of it, considering especially the Indian preponderance across its open border.

King Tribhuvan in 1950 might have offered to accede to India--like the princely States of the former British empire–but it would be unrealistic to expect his successors to be so disposed towards India. Incidentally, even in the case of most princely States in India Sardar Patel had to deploy all the skills in his statesmanly repertoire to induce the rulers to sign on the dotted line. The states' people's movement has also provided the necessary pressure from below. In some cases like Cochin in the south and Bikaner in the west, the cultural and religious affinity with the majority community in India had influenced the maharajas. Vis-a-vis Nepal, on the other hand, Indian policy makers in New Delhi and many of the ambassadors in Kathmandu had managed to dilute such cementing factors by overplaying the power dimension. No wonder King Mahendra was repelled. As the kingdom opened up and established relations with more and more countries its policies began to interact with the larger international community. If India had brought to bear on its foreign policy a regional outlook–taking the smaller South Asian neighbours into confidence–the gulf would not have widened.

There were two other reasons for King Mahendra's assertive attitude towards India, one domestic and the other geopolitical. Unreconciled to constitutional monarchy, the king set out to nip in the bud the movement for responsible government spear-headed by the Nepali Congress of B.P. Koirala. India as the source of the urge for democracy—the Socialist Party and its leaders like Ram Manohar Lohia and Jayaprakash Narayan had not only lent moral support to the Nepali Congress which was affiliated to the shortlived Asian Socialist Congress but had also tried to promote the armed struggle against the earlier Rana dispensation–was suspect in the eyes of the king and his courtiers. There were two ways in which India could have handled the situation : it could have made the king understand unmistakably that India was for the pro-democracy movement and would not brook its suppression by force. (Such a stance was feigned in the case of East Pakistan in 1971 and Sri Lanka in 1987 to justify military intervention). In the 1960s there was no question of Indian military intervention in Nepal. But India could have created world public opinion in favour of the Nepali Congress and its aspirations, tapping the immense moral resources of the socialists in and out of government in different parts of the world. King Mahendra then could not have got away with the dismissal of an elected government and detention without trial of its leader. Or, India could have formally and totally abandoned the Nepali Congress cause and stood solidly by the king, like China and Pakistan. New Delhi then would have had better leverage with the palace in Kathmandu. Instead of adopting either of these straightforward courses, India blew hot and cold trying to use the King's vulnerability as a bargaining chip in India-Nepal relations. The effort backfired.

In the process, India lost an opportunity for a principled stand in international affairs. Not even a gesture of remonstrance emanated from New Delhi when Koirala after his deposition as prime minister was gaoled for long years without trial or chargesheet and the Nepali Congress was proscribed. India which was so solicitous in 1989 of the interests of the Tamils in Sri Lanka or of the victims of the Pol Pot regime in Cambodia did not feel concerned. The immediate result was that in the wake of the 1962 Sino-Indian border conflict the Nepal king was tempted to pay India back in the same coin of expediency and Lal Bahadur Shastri had to undertake a pilgrimage to the king and appeal to King Mahendra's royal pride. Against this background when in 1989 India exuded sympathy for the advocates of a responsible government in Nepal the effort fell flat.

This brings us to an even more important factor in Nepal's new found assertiveness. With the assumption of power in China by the Communists and the disappearance of Tibet as a buffer, Nepal and other Himalayan kingdoms were directly exposed to the dynamics of the new dispensation in Beijing. Nehru had acknowledged that whenever there was a strong government in Beijing the establishment tended to be expansionist. The communist nature of the regime which had come into its own after a bitter civil strife, compounded by American intervention and the raging East-West cold war which virtually polarised the world between the belligerents, further complicated the situation. Nehru was perhaps right in recognising the irrelevance of buffer states in the twentieth century but what about the cultural autonomy of Tibet which had never been integrated into China? Did not nonalignment demand respect for the cultural autonomy of the Tibetans? Nehru did not try to promote a regional approach to China's forcible absorption of Tibet. His personal aversion for NATO blinded him to the need for collective security in a world where power was unevenly distributed. On the world scene, he joined Gamal Abdel Nasser and Josip Broz Tito in forging the nonaligned movement to limit the sway of military alliances and to ease tension between them but nearer home the autonomy of Tibet was sacrificed to appease China. Worse still, Rajiv Gandhi who tried to shine in the reflected glory of the Nehru dynasty did not have a word of sympathy for the Tibetan victims of China's military onslaught on monasteries and their occupants when he claimed to promote normalisation of Sino-Indian relations through a public relations exercise in the form of a highly personalised visit to Beijing. He had also the cheek to pour scorn over George Fernandez's courageous attempt to bring the Tibetans' struggle into world focus.[6]

One of the most perceptible results of China's emergence on the Himalayan horizon was that countries like Nepal were tempted to strike a balance between China and India, if not pit one against another. They could not also afford to affront Beijing by being close to India nor did they feel confident that India could underwrite their security even if they ceded the responsibility to New Delhi. If there had been a regional infrastructure in South Asia they could have gone along with it without appearing to side with India against China. After the 1962 border conflict between India and China--the psychological impact of which was unduly shattering with Nehru having practically gone overboard--India's smaller neighbours were not naturally impressed by its ability to safeguard their security with or without recourse to arms. The reasons for dilating at some length on India-Nepal relations against the background of China's emergence as a big power are because, in our view, the developments exposed the shortcomings of India's policies towards its neighbours, big and small. Secondly, future governments of India including the present one have to bear in mind this background to avoid repeating the mistakes or, worse still, overreacting to similar situations. But Sino-Indian relations in their various dimensions are beyond the scope of this study.

To revert to India's professed reasons for not renewing the trade and transit treaties with Nepal, the first, as already mentioned, was the alleged illfeeling of the king towards India. In other words, foreign policy making, according to Rajiv Gandhi's aides, was a campaign to make India and its leaders liked and loved by others. This was perhaps an offshoot of the comic opera of festival diplomacy indulged in by the regime at great cost to the tax payer.

The United States for several years was perhaps the least loved among the powers by the rulers of other countries but the fact did not affect the direction of its foreign policy. For instance, successive U.S. administrations perceived President de Gaulle of France as an implacable enemy of the U.S. but they did not drive France into the Soviet camp by a display of hostility. Similarly, the Soviet Union's stock in east Europe had never been high but that did not worry Moscow as long as the Warsaw Pact alliance remained intact.

The Indian foreign affairs establishment, on the other hand, dubbed the King of Nepal and the President of Sri Lanka--not to mention the former President of Pakistan--anti-Indian and went about trying to settle scores with them. It was a favourite refrain of Indian diplomats in Islamabad that General Zia-ul-Haque hated Indira Gandhi and so his overtures for normal relations with India should not be responded to. In the case of Nepal, similarly, the tendency had been to reduce inter-State relations to the level of personalities. A mature and thoughtful person like P.V. Narasimha Rao, as India's external affairs minister, had told King Birendra during a visit to Kathmandu in 1989 that the king's grandfather--King Tribhuvan--and Rajiv's grandfather were great friends and so the two grandsons should get on well ! Nepal as a monarchy might revel in dynastic glory but it will be a sad day for Indian democracy if the accident of Rajiv Gandhi's prime ministership for five years is made into a national virtue.

The second charge against the Nepal king, according to the article cited earlier, is that he advocated and stood for "equal relationship" with both India and China. The reasons for it have been already mentioned. Instead of adopting a wooden attitude that such "equal relationship" with both India and China was violative of the 1950 India-Nepal Treaty, India's effort should have been to make the relationship "more equal" towards India than towards China, which should not be difficult considering the many-sided links between the two peoples and the fact that Nepal's only outlet for most of the world is through India. China lacks both the advantages despite the Kathmandu-Kodari road. By trying to choke Nepal's links with the world India had been forcing the kingdom to move closer to, and be more dependent on, China. Pakistan in the 1960s had similarly driven Afghanistan into the Soviet lap by blocking its outlet to the world. It is relevant in this context to refer to the purchase by Nepal of anti-aircraft systems from China. According to Indian defence experts they are a potential threat to India's security. Anti-aircraft guns, however sophisticated, are defensive weapons and are reckonable only if India has intentions of violating Nepalese air space. In fact, the Nepalese publicists' justification of the transaction alluded to the Indian violation of Sri Lankan air space in 1987 and said the equipment had been acquired to prevent similar occurrences. In other words, the deal was more significant psychologically than in military terms. Zealous of its independence, Nepal will be naturally wary of allowing China a foothold in its security environment. At the same time, in the name of overcoming the presumed security threat from Nepal's acquisition of Chinese military hardware, the Indian action has exposed the entire India-Nepal border--which is open--to the danger of infiltration. India cannot man the border even if it wants to because of the financial and other costs. Thus, the security of both India and Nepal against threats from the north has to be shared and common.

The third charge against the king is that he put forward a proposal for Nepal being declared "a zone of peace" and got it endorsed by several countries, although India looked askance at it. Inherent in the foregoing in the complaint that Nepal is refusing to be a buffer between India and China. First, in the light of Nehru's rejection of the concept of buffer states, it is wrong to blame Nepal which has been historically and in effect more independent than Tibet, for refusing to be a surrogate of India. Further, the "zone of peace" idea need not affect India's interests or security if Nepal is persuaded to shield any downward push across the Himalayas. Nepal's own interests lie in fortifying its frontier to the north. It will be suicidal for Kathmandu to let the Chinese influence percolate into the plains of India in the name of settling scores with New Delhi. In the wake of the 1962 conflict also, the Nepalese leaders were very much alive to the danger of China emerging as a militarily preponderant power in the area. But if driven to the wall, the Nepalese leaders may become desperate. Statesmanship in New Delhi lies in averting such a situation and not in aggravating minor issues like two or a single treaty into *causes celebres*.

Further, with the inception of the South Asian Association for Regional Cooperation (SAARC) there could have been another avenue of reassuring Nepal on the sensitive issue of sovereign equality in practice by making a regional effort to defuse bilateral tensions. But Indian government spokesmen tirelessly chant the *mantra* that bilateral issues cannot be raised at the SAARC forum. One can understand a constraint that the institutions of a regional organisation like the SAARC will suffer in cohesion if they are used for agitating bilateral disputes among member States. But it will be unrealistic to expect Nepal to join India in any regional effort when it is the victim of a virtual economic blockade by India. Nor will Sri Lanka join an India-led chorus of platitudes in the name of SAARC when tens of thousands of Indian troops are involved in military operations against Sri Lankans on Sri Lankan soil without the approval of the government in Colombo. Interestingly, the initiative for launching SAARC was taken by Bangladesh and not India or Pakistan. It was explained in New Delhi that an Indian initiative would be misunderstood in the neighbourhood as a cover for Indian dominance by virtue of its preponderance. Similarly, a Pakistani effort in that direction could be seen by India as a move to gang up its smaller neighbours against New Delhi. Such perceptions throw light on the atmosphere in which the SAARC exercise had been undertaken. It was also a sufficient commentary on the state of India's relations with its neighbours.

After SAARC came into being the effort has been to keep it as a debating society for hammering out consensus statements on innocuous subjects plus an additional source of sinecures for foreign service officials, capped by an annual ceremonial called meeting of the heads of government. All these three avocations of the regional organisation are desirable because jaw-jaw on the perils of terrorism or the need for immunisation of children in the member-States is better than a war of words from the establishments and their compliant media. Secondly, the more the career opportunities for Foreign Service bureaucrats the greater the prospects of keeping disputes in check. Finally, it is good for leaders of the different neighbouring countries to meet once a year within the geographical region and break bread with each other. But this is not regional approach, not by a long chalk. It should provide for informal means of sorting out disputes and defusing tensions within the region with a view to forging a shared outlook on international issues. The Organisation of African Unity, despite the many challenges faced by it, is striving to be such an organisation. But India does not let SAARC grow into such a useful institution.

Another sacred cow of the Indian external affairs establishment is the 1950 Indo-Nepalese Treaty. The treaty was made for the mutual benefit of the signatory countries in the circumstances prevailing forty years ago. It is not the Bible or the *Bhagavadgita* nor can its provisions be immutable like the Marxian gospel for hindsighted communists. But Indian diplomats and their apologists in the academy think that India and Nepal have been made for the treaty and not the treaty for the countries. It was depressing to see an enlightened person like P.V. Narasimha Rao extol in the Lok Sabha the sanctity of the 1950 treaty as the handiwork of Nehru's time. But it is not so sacrosanct as to warrant a cold war with Nepal to keep its letter intact after the spirit has evaporated and the need is being felt for its revision to suit the new geopolitical situation. The Rajiv Government, blinded by pride and prejudice and flush with an ever growing arsenal of sophisticated weapons, could not see the wood for the trees. It was widely believed that because the then Prime Minister's wife was not accorded in Kathmandu the kind of welcome which was her due Nepal had been marked down for tough treatment. Apart from such egotistic tendencies of the rulers, the malaise as far as India's relations with its neighbours are concerned is deeper and flows from a failure at the dawn of independence itself to develop a rational and realistic perspective on relations with States in the immediate neighbourhood. Nehru's pre-Independence writings talked of a confederation of Asian States on the assumption that Asianism would be a driving force in the wake of decolonisation of the continent. After Independence, Nehru's thinking and effort were concentrated on playing the role of a honest broker on the larger global scene as a result of which India had no doubt benefited by acquiring a larger than life image notwithstanding its military weakness and industrial backwardness. Nehru forged it into a psychological weapon to safeguard India's interests against possible depredations by the big powers and for keeping the cold war away from Indian shores. India's economic development was also promoted by securing support for it from both East and West. But in the process the problems in the neighbourhood and the problems involving Indian settlers in other Asian and African countries went by the board.

Indira Gandhi had used international relations largely as a means of buttressing her sense of personal security which, in her perception, had been under constant threat from politicians at home, leaders of neighbouring countries and the ubiquitous "foreign hand." For her son and political heir foreign affairs was an opportunity for junkets abroad and reading out speeches written by foreign office hacks. He had neither the vision nor the understanding necessary to evolve durable relations with neighbours. The deference which characterised his attitude towards the Big Powers and even China turned into arrogance and posturing when dealing with smaller States. For instance, during his first visit as prime minister to the U.S. in 1985 Rajiv Gandhi was so obsequious in his behaviour that Ronald Reagan was moved to grant his wish for the release of Mohammad Yunus Khan's son serving a prison term there for drug smuggling and other offences. While in Beijing more recently he did not have the nerve to demand China's recognition of Sikkim's status as an Indian State in return for Indian abandonment of the cause of Tibetan autonomy. Against this background, it will be a Herculean task for the Vishwanath Pratap Singh government to put foreign relations on a pedestal of principled dealings with powers big and small.

## Pakistan

At the dawn of independence, the Indian government leadership, perhaps preoccupied with the aftermath of partition, was obsessed with Pakistan. Theories were propounded that, unable to find its identity, Pakistan would either disintegrate or end up in the lap of an external power. In either case, the consequences for India would have been undesirable and so the government should have tried to carry Pakistan along with it and develop a relationship based on mutual trust. The Pakistani leadership, both civilian and military, was no doubt hell bent on projecting India as an implacable enemy but there were elements in Pakistan who stood for amicable relations with India and who also had a stake in India-Pakistan amity. The then Pakistan province of East Pakistan--today's Bangladesh--had a vested interest in improved India-Pakistan relations because it would enable it to resist West Pakistani or Punjabi dominance. The migrants from India, called Mohajirs, had a nostalgic attachment for India partly because many of their kith and kin still lived in India. The civilians as distinct from the military with its growing political ambitions also favoured amicable ties with India because it would partly deprive the military and the hot heads of a plank to climb on to seize power. For instance, in 1961, in the wake of Field Marshal Ayub Khan's seizure of power, Begum Shah Nawaz who was a family friend of Nehru told one of us that she had entreated Nehru when he was in Lahore for the signing of the Indus Waters Treaty to treat Pakistan in such a way that moderate elements could assert themselves there. The Pakistani military with its Punjabi dominance was circumspect enough to avoid a showdown with India until its military muscle was beefed up with U.S. supplies but it needed India-Pakistan tension to thrive.

The Indian leadership and its experts had no eye for such a perspective on India-Pakistan relations. While a section of the people transferred their distrust of Indian Muslims into hostility for Pakistan, the leadership had imprisoned itself in a web of anti-Pakistanism. For instance, the intervention of the World Bank--and the U.S. as an unseen prompter--had become necessary for

India and Pakistan to agree on an equitable division of the waters of the Indus river common to both countries. Article 51 of the Indian Constitution clearly provided for settlement of international disputes by arbitration but the Indian government did not take the initiative in the matter. India as a leading nonaligned country was preaching to all and sundry to avoid conflict, lessen tension and settle disputes amicably but in its prime test of foreign policy it failed to live up to those principles. True, Pakistan had been spoiling for tension and worse with India but India reciprocated in kind. Otherwise, as Gorbachev has demonstrated by his attitude to the U.S. and West Europe on a number of East-West issues including arms control, statesmanship if not generosity by one of the parties brings down the temperature and defuses crises. India itself during Rajiv Gandhi's prime ministership had done it when an adventurist tactic by the military had brought India and Pakistan to the brink of another conflict. But that was a negative gesture taken at the eleventh hour. For instance, after the Karachi ceasefire agreement of 1949, India could have taken the initiative for a political settlement of the Kashmir issue instead of allowing it to fester sub-continental relations to this day. But the argument of the policy makers and their apologists was that any such gesture would fortify the Ayub dictatorship in Pakistan. It was nothing but an alibi because India-Pakistan hostility had earlier helped the military to put the politicians in the wrong and seize power. It was in that context that Pakistani liberals like Begum Shah Nawaz, Mian Iftikhar-ud-Din and even Faiz Ahmed Faiz had pleaded with Nehru for "generosity" on Kashmir. Sheikh Mohammed Abdullah within Kashmir and Jayaprakash Narayan and others in the rest of India had also advocated a political settlement of Kashmir on the basis of give and take. But Nehru did not wake up until in the wake of the 1962 Indian border conflict with China. Zulfiquar Ali Bhutto thought American pressure would make India yield and tried to drive a hard bargain. Bhutto, too, had no interest in settling India-Pakistan disputes because that would rob him of a handle against Ayub Khan and thus deprive him of an opportunity for easy political advancement.

The result of Indian obduracy or failure to act was that internally Pakistan had been doomed to long spells of military dictatorship interspersed by bouts of opportunism under leaders like Bhutto, while internationally Pakistan had been driven first into the U.S. camp and then into the Chinese embrace. The region opened up for intervention by external actors as well as the extension of cold war tension. As mentioned earlier, Pakistan might have been plagued by an identity problem which drove it into such calamities but India had no need for a fixation involving Pakistan as a permanent enemy. The tragedy was that with the new generations of Indians growing up with a perception of undying Pakistani hostility for India and with Hindu-Muslim relations within India also vitiated by external dimensions--like inflow of petro-dollars from West Asia for Muslim clergy and extremists and aversion for the Central government by Kashmiris taking the shape of pro-Pakistani gestures--relations with Pakistan became a tool of power politics within India. This was amply demonstrated during Rajiv Gandhi's prime ministership. For three years from 1985 Rajiv Gandhi had ignored or rebuffed General Zia-ul-Haque's overtures for confidence building measures between the two governments like conclusion of a no-war pact, agreement to avoid attacks on each other's nuclear installations and mutual and balanced reduction of forces. An oral accord on immunity for nuclear facilities from military attacks by either country remained unconsummated as long as Zia remained the ruler. Then in a flush of enthusiasm for the restoration of the democratic processes in Pakistan and the assumption of prime ministership by Benazir Bhutto, the Rajiv Gandhi establishment nearly went overboard by promptly converting the accord into a formal agreement and by agreeing to bring back the Simla Agreement of 1972 as the basis for India-Pakistan relations, setting aside the tortuous negotiations for three years for a no-war pact or a treaty of peace and friendship. The effort especially on the Indian Government side was cosmetic, to project the prime minister as a supporter of democracy in Pakistan and reap the electoral support of Muslim voters in India. More substantial issues like mutual and balanced force reduction to enable both governments to scale down their military budgets and exchange of data on nuclear installations for the treaty to be operative were relegated to the back burner. The honeymoon with Pakistan had also come in handy to impress the Chinese leadership during Rajiv Gandhi's subsequent trip to Beijing that India was keen to improve relations with its neighbours especially Pakistan which has been China's informal ally. Sound international relations cannot be built on such quick sands for short-term power political benefits.

Against this background, let us recall both the negative and positive factors in the India-Pakistan relationship. The major negative factors are:

(1) Powerful individuals and forces in both countries with a vested interest in maintaining unfriendly relations between India and Pakistan. They are capable of queering the pitch whenever a sincere attempt is made to mend the fences and bring the two countries closer. They belong to political parties, the bureaucracy, the media and the armed forces. The most striking in this respect is the crusade of Benazir Bhutto's political adversaries in Pakistan against her so-called softness towards India. The alliance of opposition parties called the Islamic Democratic Alliance headed by the Punjab chief minister, Mian Nawaz Sharif, has been charging the Pakistan government with having accepted Indian dominance in the region. Benazir Bhutto, for her part, has been demanding Indian withdrawal from the Siachin glacier on the ground that the Simla Agreement had made the line of control in Kashmir inviolable and, also privately, that such an Indian gesture to the spirit of the Simla agreement would reinforce her position vis-a-vis her critics. On the sensitive question of Pakistani involvement with terrorists in Indian Punjab and Kashmir she shrugs off responsibility implying it was the handiwork of the Zia period intelligence outfit, the Inter-Services Intelligence (ISI). Indian officials and journalists also buy the theory in an effort to justify in retrospect Rajiv Gandhi's handling of relations with Pakistan. Besides the political factor described above, historical, religious and ideological reasons account for the negative approach especially in Pakistan to better relations between the two countries.

(2) On the Indian side, there are some elements who clamour for Akhand Hindustan implying the undoing of Pakistan. But even the lunatic fringe among such extremists does not seriously visualise the coming together of India, Pakistan and Bangladesh to re-form the subcontinent. The emergence of the Bharatiya Janata Party (BJP) as a force in north India is also a damper to any serious move in that direction because the party has a pragmatic approach to India-Pakistan relations. In fact, the founder of the Bharatiya Jan Sangh which was a forerunner of the BJP, Dr. Shyama Prasad Mukerjee, had parted company with the old Hindu Mahasabha on the issue of Akhand Bharat. Nevertheless, the Indian military intervention in 1971 in the East Pakistan crisis and the pro-Pakistan upsurge in Kashmir have been promoting anti-Pakistan elements in India. In some cases, antipathy for Muslims at home--for a variety of reasons–also assumes the shape of anti-Pakistanism which gets reinforced as a backlash to separatist tendencies among Indian Muslims.

(3) On the Pakistan side, there is fear and apprehension that too close a relationship with India might in the long run weaken the distinctive identity of Pakistan as an Islamic state and undo the efforts of Bhutto and his successors to deepen Pakistan's relations with the Islamic community in West Asia. To counter and pre-empt such a possibility they feel the necessity of sharpening the image of Pakistan as a blue-blooded Islamic state distinct from "Hindu India."

(4) The continuance of Kashmir as a source of discord despite the Tashkent Declaration of 1966 and the Simla Agreement of 1972. The problem is aggravated when there is tension between the two governments on other issues, while it persists as a source of ill feeling between the two peoples. There is no point in ignoring this fact of life. It is both necessary and possible to evolve a workable solution on the basis of mutual accommodation of each other's security and political interests and without the involvement of external agencies so that it is not handed down to the 21st century as an unhappy legacy of bungling by the leaders of the two countries in the last fifty years.

Any conscious and sincere effort to develop friendly relations between India and Pakistan will involve countering and overcoming the negative factors listed above. Both countries have to strive in that direction. At the same time, it is realistic to recognise that factors which spur urges for reunion of the two Germanys do not exist in the India-Pakistan context and that there should be no serious thought of a confederal or federal arrangement between the two sovereign States. Also, the positive factors in favour of India-Pakistan amity will be jeopardised by unfounded zeal for larger structural changes. The positive factors are :

(1) The common experience that whenever average Indians and Pakistanis meet there is always a spontaneous exchange of goodwill and friendship. Those who had gone through the trauma of partition and its horrendous aftermath are fading away and the new generations of Indians and Pakistanis are not plagued by such painful memories. They also do not suffer from nostalgia for the pre-partition period like their forbears. So they can start on a clean slate. There is profound curiosity among the younger generations about each other's countries and peoples and a sense of kinship in the cultural sphere, especially cinema, the theatre and music. There is no doubt that the overwhelming majority of people in both countries wants good and friendly relations between the two countries.

(2) If tension is reduced and an atmosphere of trust is created, both governments can substantially reduce their needless and wasteful military expenditure. The National Front government should be able to respond to the Pakistani suggestion for mutual and balanced reduction of armed forces by both countries in the ratio of one to three between Pakistan and India. Either Government should take the other into confidence before enlarging its military forces or adding to their arsenals. The scarce resources thus saved would be useful in ameliorating the lot of the people in both countries. Psychologically also, such a measure will help create a new atmosphere of trust.

(3) Close economic relationship will be beneficial to both countries. Coordination of trade policies can bring down the prices of imported goods for both. The Pakistani perception that the better developed Indian economy might swamp its fledgling industries can be dispelled by bringing complementarity to bear on the industrial and trade policies of the two governments.

(4) If the 1940s was the decade of partition of countries--Germany, the Indian subcontinent, Palestine and Korea, among others--the last decade has witnessed a new atmosphere of understanding and even reconciliation between the States formed out of divided countries. This is a global phenomenon and we in India and Pakistan cannot be impervious to its benign influence. At the same time, as stated earlier, formal reunion of States is less important than cordial relations between them and it is both wrong and premature to expect the situation in East and West Germany to be automatically replicated elsewhere. Nevertheless, the phenomenon of neighbours like France and West Germany, sworn enemies until 1945 with a record of invasions and bloody wars getting closer and promoting regional cohesion within the European Community should not be overlooked. There can be no permanent enemies nor need mutual interests between countries remain perennially conflicting.

India and Pakistan have everything to gain and nothing to lose by being friends and good neighbours. The acquisition of military hardware by one will cease to be seen as a threat by the other if a system of mutual and balanced force reduction is evolved between the two countries. Economies and trade policies can also be complementary. A system of mutual consultation and constant dialogue can reduce frictions in the realm of international relations. India's preponderance in many respects will not be perceived by Pakistan as a means of regional dominance but can be availed of by it for mutual and regional benefit. In such a scheme of things, the governments of the two countries will have to play the most important role. But it is too vital a matter to be left entirely to the moods and mores of political leaders and their civil service establishments. There has to be a movement at the people's level in both countries to promote such a desirable consummation. The recent restoration of the democratic process in Pakistan and the withdrawal of Soviet troops from Afghanistan have been positive developments. The assumption of office by the National Front government in India can take advantage of the new favourable situation to lead the region to an era of understanding and shared progress.

**Sri Lanka**

The direct Indian involvement in Sri Lanka's ethnic conflict compounded by intervention by the military has brought into focus issues which are relevant to all South Asian countries. All countries especially in our region have problems of minorities--religious, ethnic or racial. Such problems can be solved only on the basis of equality and justice for the minorities. Reluctance to do so or use of force to cow down the minorities will only complicate the issues. leading to strife, violence and intervention by outsiders. It is often very difficult to solve the problems to the satisfaction of the minorities but once the necessary trust is established the minorities can be drawn into the mainstream of national life. In the case of Sri Lanka successive governments not only failed to do so but also adopted a policy of discrimination against the Tamils.

(2) Sometimes the problem of the minorities spills over into neighbouring countries to grow into inter-State problems. It happened in Sri Lanka when a veritable genocide of the Tamils by the Sinhala security forces of the government caused an influx of hundreds of thousands of refugees into India. But direct Indian involvement in the conflict had introduced a new dimension without helping the solution of the basic issue of security and equality of the Tamils. Nationalist feeling was aroused among the Sinhalese first and a section of the Tamil militants later. This was despite the legal sanction of the intervention in the form of an agreement between the heads of the Indian and Sri Lankan Governments.

(3) In the conditions which prevailed in Sri Lanka in 1984-85 it was understandable for the Tamil minority to seek as much

assistance as possible from outside. At the same time a country not having equable relations with its neighbour feels tempted in such situations to increase its clout by encouraging and assisting the minorities' struggle. In the perception of most Sri Lankans, that was what had happened when India used the opportunity to intervene militarily. It has proved counterproductive. The refusal over the years of the Sinhala majority in Sri Lanka to concede and respect the legitimate rights of the Tamil minority within the framework of Sri Lanka sovereignty resulted in the Tamil demand for a separate sovereign state of their own. It encouraged those in India who would like this country to play the role of a "gendany" in the region to move in. Their dream has now been shattered when, after paying a heavy price in terms of deaths and injuries to Indian soldiers as well as Sri Lankan citizens and a crippling financial outlay, the Indian army is being withdrawn from a ravaged territory without any assurance that peace will prevail there and that Tamil interests will be safeguarded. India's relations with Sri Lanka have to be considered *de novo* because the island is now on the verge of a new political dispensation which will not be, on the whole, favourable to India, at least for some time.

The clear lesson is that even if a country supports the legitimate interests of a minority in another country it will alienate the majority which constitutes the government and thus aggravates inter-State tension. India's Sri Lankan experience has once again proved that only adherence to basic values and principles such as equity and justice to the minorities and non-interference in other countries' domestic affairs can help create an atmosphere of understanding and amity among nations.

India has to assure its neighbours that it has no hegemonistic ambitions of a "regional super power". Behaving like a Big Brother is not a workable proposition in our time. Because of India's direct involvement in Sri Lanka it will take many years to overcome suspicions regarding India's intentions not only in relation to that island but also towards other smaller neighbours. If Sri Lanka survives its present ordeal it will be so alive to the "Indian threat" that normal relations between the two countries will be difficult to restore. If, on the other hand, the unhappy island succumbs to the unending civil strife and distintegrates India will have a hornets' nest on its hands. Even gaining military control of the north-eastern parts of Sri Lanka will not help, assuming that India can get away with such an adventure.

## SAARC

SAARC which has been already weakened by the India-Sri Lanka dispute will be further eroded as an instrument of regional cooperation. It will be India versus the rest of South Asia. Military muscle alone will not buy security in such a situation. The long open border with Nepal cannot be secured if a hostile Nepal tries to spite India. Strife-torn Sri Lanka will affect the peace and security of India's southern coast line. Already Punjab and Kashmir are in turmoil. This is not a scenario for progress and security of India even if it earns the dubious distinction of a regional super power. Above all, with the diplomatic weapon having been blunted, India's relations with all the South Asian neighbours will have to be governed more by military means and less by diplomacy. If the reaction of the Congress-I and its supporters to the National Front government's initiatives to normalise relations with the neighbours is an index the tendency will be to take a "tough line" instead of trying to iron out differences diplomatically.

The thinking behind these flawed policies is derived from exploded concepts. For instance, it is claimed that smaller States in the vicinity of larger and more powerful ones cannot afford the luxury of autonomy in international affairs but must learn to live with the "security concerns" of the stronger States. The Soviet Union until the 1980s enforced the discredited "Brezhnev doctrine" on its east European neighbours with results which are becoming explicit today. It would arrogate to itself the power to dictate to its neighbours in the west the level of armaments they should possess and put its troops on the soil of its surrogate States to force them to do so. The controversy over American nuclear missiles in western Europe arose from such Soviet policies. Once Mikhail Gorbachev realised the folly of the policy and waived the objection, the missiles became redundant paving the way for successful arms control negotiations and enabling the Europeans to breathe freely. In the process, global tension too has eased considerably with headway being made in the settlement of problems in West Asia and Africa.

Implicit in the foregoing critique of the handling of India's relations with its South Asian neighbours by the earlier regimes, especially that of Rajiv Gandhi, are the bases for a sound alternate policy. Its emphasis should be on a regional approach so that bilateral incompatibilities within the region are ironed out. A country like India, large in size and population, militarily strong and with a great industrial potential could, if it reconciled its differences with its neighbours, promote the progress and security of the entire region. Otherwise, it will suffer along with them as a result of ill conceived efforts to impose its will on others. The launching of the SAARC showed great promise of regional cooperation but more recent developments have been a damper.

Unlike in the 1950s, the regional approach has been tried with success elsewhere. The European Community is a glaring example, despite initial British reservations. From an economic union it has grown into a political grouping adopting a coordinated stand on international issues like Palestine and East-West detente. It also displays a shared concern for the security of the whole region. ASEAN is another success story, though more modest. Indonesia and Malaysia which had been at loggerheads and were caught in a cold war have now joined the other ASEAN members in shaping the security and foreign policies of the whole of South-East Asia. Even the Organisation of African Unity is able to sort out disputes among member States without a Sri Lankan type of situation developing in the region.

The SAARC could take after them. The presence in the region of a large State like India need not come in the way of the SAARC developing cohesion if the present government of India learns from the mistakes of its predecessors. This is both an opportunity and challenge for the V.P. Singh government.

(Based on a discussion paper written for the Indian Centre for Democratic Socialism.)

## *Notes and References*

1. A television "think" programme in January 1990 paraded journalists and others cautioning the new foreign minister against reviewing Rajiv Gandhi's policies towards India's neighbours on the ground that external powers would fill the "vacuum" caused by a change in India's forward policies.
2. When in the middle of 1989 President Premadasa of Sri Lanka demanded withdrawal of Indian troops from the island pro-Establishment Indian newspapers threatened the island with the fate of Cyprus or Lebanon, the choice being benignly left to its President.
3. *Perestroika, New thinking for our county and the world,"* New York, Harper and Row, 1987.
4. It was said that the Nepal king had not treated Mrs. Sonia Gandhi as she should have been during a visit to Kathmandu.
5. S.D. Muni, Strategic Analysis, Vol. xii, No. iv, IDSA, New Delhi.
6. The reference is to Rajiv Gandhi's criticism in Parliament of Fernandes's moral initiative on Tibet.

# 8

## *Vox Populi*

M.L. Ahuja

The dawn of 1990 brought a mixed feeling of hope, joy and apprehension to the common man in India. A new government at the Centre had just emerged. The joy was in the peaceful transition at the top political level. The common man had reasserted himself that a government must deserve the support it carried. But the emergence of a minority government, in the light of the failure of Janata Government (1977-79) raised the question: how long will this government last?

The eighties had seen agonising spells of an ascending price graph and continuing violence - with mounting social tensions and agitations. It was during this period, dominated successively by the Nehru dynasty that corruption in public life had become a central issue, "beginning with the alleged sale of the army's aging Centurion tanks to parties close to Israel and South Africa, the Thal-Viashet deal, the Kuo oil deal, the Ferranti deal, the HDW submarine contract, the Antulay affair and the Bofors deal"[1]. All of them became subjects of debate within and outside Parliament. The change of government evoked a sigh of relief on that score. "We will bring to the people of India a new programme of action to be implemented within a specified time-frame". These words of V.P. Singh, the new prime minister, in his first broadcast, brought a fresh breeze to the common man.

While the man in the street doesn't expect the government to wield a magic wand and turn everything into gold, he certainly expects a clean, honest and efficient administration. He wants a peaceful, secure life and expects a friendly attitude from the police and a minimum of civic amenities, a helpful bureaucracy, and availability of the essential means of livelihood at reasonable prices. In 1984, he was promised such an administration. But, what he actually got was a continuing stink of corruption, arrogance of power and a blatant disregard of his hopes and aspirations. Following his exit from the union cabinet in April 1987 V.P. Singh launched a mass-contact campaign which took him to several States. During his seven years of association with the Congress government, first as chief minister of Uttar Pradesh (1980-83) and later as a central minister holding in turn the important portfolios of commerce, finance and defence, he was rated as a highly intelligent and competent administrator. Thus, the vote for him was undeniably a vote for change.

No doubt, Rajiv's first years in government had been marked by a number of initiatives, starting with the anti-defection law. He pushed for a clean public life, tried to induct new blood into the Congress (I) and addressed himself to the problems in Punjab, Assam and Mizoram. He reorganised and trimmed some of the ministries, streamlined and speeded up the functioning of the government and re-trained the mammoth bureaucracy. In the economic sphere, he liberalised the industrial and trade regimes and pushed towards modernistation of the economy. A glorious India of twenty-first century was his dream. A new education policy was prepared and introduced, the family planning drive was restarted laying stress on anti-poverty programmes. But very soon the termites of indiscipline, corruption and sycophancy began to eat into the political edifice with dangerous consequences. Thus, if Rajiv was the creature of tragic happenings, Singh was a way out of mass frustration. He has already been rated as a man of principles. More than anything else it was his apparent uprightness that brought him to the pinnacle.

Terrorism and communal violence became rampant particularly during the later years of the Rajiv regime. Safety and security of men, women and children, to whatever community they may belong, were not assured. In some areas, like Punjab and Jammu

& Kashmir, life became a nightmare. Communal disturbances signified that the grievances and fears of sections of the community had no other way to being ventilated Why is it that the communal virus has become a veritable epidemic? First, education right from the primary level had not been properly oriented for inculcating a secular bias and secondly the Government's preventive or punitive action came too late in the day and it was too little to deter the trouble-makers. This has been vividly summed up by Prof. Khalid Mahmud in the following words :

> The phenomenon of Congress (I)'s decline is not merely confined to fall in mass support or degeneration of its organisational moorings; in a wider sense it signifies a 'crisis in credibility'. The once mighty political machine has become unproductive in terms of leadership and performance and its ability to deliver the goods is suspect in the public eye ... Marred by erratic decision-making, false starts, public scandals and successive debacles, his (Rajiv Gandhi's) style of functioning is said to be anti-climax to the charismatic bearing of the Nehru dynasty.[2]

Before coming to power, V.P. Singh had led a campaign against corruption in public life. He promised true democracy instead of the fake one in operation. He also advocated rule of law without which there cannot be a truly people's government. The Janata government (1977-79) collapsed because of excessive personal ambitions of some of the top leaders. Structurally the National Front is almost akin to the Janata Party. But the bitter echoes of the Janata experience should make the National Front wiser. The leadership also should understand that its future depends on performance. The stupendous tasks that lie ahead require continuous involvement of the masses in overcoming the problems.

Fortunately for the common man, the V.P. Singh government started on a promising note. The government took up the promised reforms with earnestness and unbelievable speed. The 11-day first session of the ninth Lok Sabha proved fruitful. The government's "Action Plan" showed its determination to forge ahead. Its scope is indeed comprehensive touching all aspects of the country's social and economic life.

The time-bound programmes, announced in quick succession, are its redeeming features. Practically every day there is hopeful news. This should endear the government to the masses and should make them believe that the leadership is in for a much longer tenure than the few weeks that Rajiv Gandhi and his coterie were inclined to allow it.

Among its notable initiatives within a month of its assuming power are efforts to arrive at the truth in respect of the Bofors kickbacks with a view to bringing the guilty persons to book. The appointment of Lok Pal, having jurisdiction over the council of ministers, including the prime minister, to tackle corruption at higher political levels, is proposed in the Lok Pal Bill 1989, introduced in the Ninth Lok Sabha on December 29, 1989. To meet a long-felt need a national security council has been announced. Since there had been a number of supersessions in the past raising doubts about the independence of the judiciary, and since the final guarantor of the citizen's rights is not the Constitution but the personality and intellectual integrity of the judiciary, a national judicial commission has been announced. This commission will look after the appointments and transfer of the supreme court and high court judges. This freedom of the judiciary, it has been felt, will enable the judges to conduct themselves in a manner befitting public confidence.

Politicians have been encouraging encroachment on public land using clusters of *jhuggis* as as vote banks. This has led to the proliferation of slums exposing the citizens to the hazards of fire and epidemic. The government is conscious of its responsibility to safeguard public lands and to maintain the norms of the master plan and municipal regulations. At the same time, it has to be sensitive to human considerations, particularly in relation to the most disadvantaged section of the people residing in the slums. The government has therefore decided on an urban development policy. According to it;

1. No established *jhuggis* which are already inhabited will be removed until a plan for their rehabilitation is finalised. Putting up of fresh jhuggis will, however, be prevented.

2. The emphasis will be on prevention. All land owning agencies have been advised to take steps to prevent encroachment on public land.

3. Removal action in respect of encroachments, unauthorised constructions and unauthorised colonies will be taken right at the initial stages.

4. Firm action will be taken against unauthorised constructions of a commercial nature.

The government has also embarked on steps to check inflation. It has also taken steps to enlarge and strengthen the public distribution system. Excessive secrecy and deliberate denial of information to the public on vital matters affecting the nation have, in the past, led to arbitrariness on the part of the executive. Openness in government functioning promised by the National Front will thus promote a better appreciation by the public of what the government intends to do and also makes the government accountable. In this context, amendment of the Official Secrets Act to enable easy access to information is a step in the right direction. Similarly, repeal of the Postal Bill will safeguard the citizen's right to privacy. The withholding of vital information from the people regarding commissions of enquiry is sought to be checked through another change in the law.

Power had been concentrated at the Centre in an overwhelming manner and the State leaders and even chief ministers were reduced to mere factotums whose fate, both immediate and long-term, depended on the high command. As the Congress (I)'s grip on the States weakened regional parties and regional leaders emerged. Punjab especially witnessed the most debilitating and dangerous situation where Jarnail Singh Bhindranwale, propped by the Congress (I) to counter the Akalis, transformed into an ominous spectre that refused to be buried to date. The governments in opposition-ruled States were frequently toppled by the Centre which assumed direct control of them in the name of President's rule. The National Front government is committed to reshape Centre-State relations on a federal basis.

Corruption in the administration has its root cause in the increasingly high cost of elections which also witnessed the use of muscle power. This is sought to be countered through comprehensive electoral reform.

In Jammu & Kashmir, the phenomenon of latent political discontent spilling into the streets took a violent form. The State government having lost its credibility was unable to cope with the situation. In the extraordinary circumstances, the Centre could not be a silent spectator. It was left with no soft options and had to act firmly. The State governor, General Krishna Rao was replaced by Jagmohan, keeping in mind the latter's intimate knowledge of the state and his administrative acumen in handling explosive situations. It is nevertheless an unpalatable decision for the Centre as the party's rank and file doesn't seem to be in favour of it. But it has come as a big relief to those who want restoration of peace and tranquility in the Valley. During his earlier tenure as governor (1984-88) Jagmohan had established cordial ties with the people. It was during his tenure that an effort was made to provide a clean administration to the State. But for reasons best known to him, Farooq Abdullah resigned "in protest" against the induction of Jagmohan as governor. His assertion that he has not been consulted doesn't seem to be credible. The administration will have to isolate the militants from the mainstream of Kashmiris and the Valley cleansed for democratic functioning.

Till May 1987, when Surjit Singh Barnala's Government was dismissed in Punjab, the previous government's policy was to abandon the use of force and invoke the democratic process to secure peace. The accord with Longowal in July 1985 marked the beginning of the new phase of reconciliation with the alienated Sikhs and Rajiv Gandhi's initiative was hailed by the media as a "hopeful signal", the lifting of the cloud of uncertainty and anxiety", a "blueprint of peace" and a "victory for all". It was in pursuance of the spirit of "compromise and accommodation" that elections were held for State assembly in September 1985 and the Akali Dal government was installed in office.

But by making a deal with the Congress government the moderate Akalis incurred the wrath of young militants who denounced them as traitors to the Sikh cause. Despite having swept the polls, the Akali leadership became unpopular. The Centre dismissed the Akali government for its alleged failure to combat terrorism and imposed President's rule.

Subsequent events showed that the Government was unable to chart out a credible and effective course of action. Repressive laws with sweeping powers to the State were enacted. Neverthless, terrorism continued unabated and an environment of fear, insecurity and uncertainty prevailed.

A mini Operation Bluestar in May 1988 resulted in the surrender of 151 terrorists and the slaying of 109 others. The President's rule was extended and the Constitution amended, empowering the Centre to proclaim emergency, if it deemed necessary, but the killing spree still continued. An end to terrorism was nowhere in sight. On the contrary, the militant ranks swelled on account of an increasing number of young persons joining the extremists.

In this context, the V.P. Singh government's greatest breakthrough has been in getting the different Akali leaders to the negotiating table. An all-party meeting was arranged and a rally was organised at Ludhiana. Two days before the rally Simranjit Singh Mann had talks with V.P. Singh and other National Front leaders in Delhi. But the mysterious death of an Akali (Mann) M.P., J.S. Khudian, was a setback. While the police have been made to stop repressive measures the terrorists have become bolder. Their prime target during the last two months has been the security personnel.

The new administration's first task, therefore, is to evolve a consensus among the parties and restore faith in the administration. Until that happens, bloodshed, anguish and suspicion will continue. V.P. Singh's visit to the golden temple in Amritsar soon after assuming power provided a healing touch and established his government's credibility in the eyes of both the Sikhs and the Hindus. Failure to act against those who participated in the anti-Sikh killings of 1984 was an obstacle in the way of the solution of the Punjab problem. Therefore, setting up of special courts to try persons involved in the 1984 riots, rehabilitation of Sikh army deserters, judicial probe into the death of Khudian, and review of cases against persons charged with minor offences are welcome steps.

In short, the government's earnestness to solve many of the problems facing the country is praiseworthy. There is, however, need to draw comprehensive guidelines at all levels to ensure that there is no gap between precept and practice. It is generally the non-action at the bureaucratic level that brings a bad name to the government. Setting up of consultative committees at the grass-roots level is a remedy.

It is a truism that the youth has to transform India from its present sorry plight to a vibrant and vigilant democracy. By and large, young men and women have been losing confidence in the top leaders. Because of frustration among the youth, unethical trends have emerged with a vengeance. The deterioration in the standard of youth is due to the state of the education. The young people are being drawn into anti-social practices. The new government has to enable them to develop their personality and make the country a better place to live in.

The new government must also eliminate flatterers and sycophants. Such people distort the values and concepts which lie at the base of official policies. Then there are endless social evils - child marriages, dowry, bride burnings, etc. Violence against the weaker sections of society by powerful landlords, goondas, and mafia has to be tackled effectively. The government should see to it that the people of all classes, urban and rural, educated and uneducated, the elite, the intelligentsia and others, regardless of their political affiliations, live with dignity and pride.

The menace of poll rigging and other electoral malpractices has also to be eradicated without fear and favour.

V.P. Singh's government, no doubt, is a minority government. Its position is decidedly fragile, since it is supported by political parties with contradictory ideologies. But, its policy of securing a national consensus on vital issues affecting the country should ultimately pay dividends. A sense of participation is perceptible from the pronouncements of the ruling party as well as the left and right parties. This should certainly contribute to the government's stability and popularity. The previous government lost its credibility as the leadership believed in coterie rule. On the other hand, V.P. Singh's technique of meeting people and chalking out programmes after thorough discussions and consultations with leaders of various shades of opinion ensures a pragmatic approach to problems.

However, its future depends upon its performance and not on high sounding pronouncements which were the hallmark of Rajiv Gandhi's regime. The new government has to win and retain the people's confidence. That is what the common man expects.

## *References*

1. Subhabrata Bhattacharya, "Decade of Crisis and Hope", *Hindustan Times*, 31 December 1989.
2. Prof. Khalid Mahmud, "The Sikh Problem : Failure of the Process", *Indian Political Scene 1989*, Instt. of Regional Studies, Islamabad, p.255.

# *Appendices*

## Appendix I

# *Broadcast to the Nation*

*The following is the text of Vishwanath Pratap Singh's broadcast on 3 December 1989 after assumption of prime ministership.*

Dear Countrymen,

It was only a few days back that we were amidst you seeking your mandate. We sought you out on the highways and the lanes and bylanes of our villages and cities. It will be my endeavour that the government structures do not come in the way of the dialogue we have established. We have brought to this capital city the dust of the fields and granaries of India. Its message will guide us in everything that we do.

Delhi may glitter, but millions of Indian homes are without the light of hope. The voice of the government will be the voice of such homes and the voice of peasants, workers and the youth. If power is a sword, it will be wielded on behalf of the poor and toiling masses.

The people of India have made a major contribution in the struggle for change in the last few years. For this, I am grateful to you. On behalf of the National Front and the Janata Dal, I thank the Left parties and the BJP for extending support to the new government for the new challenges that are before us.

After a long and dark night, the day had dawned but it is still a misty dawn. The coffers of the government are empty. Our hearts are inflamed. There has been much violence and bloodshed. Inflation had impoverished our people. But, we have had two main strengths---your faith and our fortitude. It is these strengths which have enabled us to succeed in our difficult struggle, and they alone will again enable us to forge ahead on our chosen path.

We will try to solve the burning problems of the nation through consensus and reconciliation. The opposition will also be taken into confidence. India belongs to all of us and all must work for her progress.

The agony of Punjab continues. While separatism is no answer to our problems, there is an urgent need for a national endeavour to resolve the problem. A national effort will be made to resolve the complex problems like Punjab, J&K and Ram Janmabhoomi / Babri masjid issues.

Riots and violence have shaken us, but we should not forget that our greatest strength is our emotional oneness. We will not allow this to be weakened. A nation is not a map on a piece of paper. It lives in the hearts of the people. And if hearts are divided, the nation is divided. We will not allow this to happen. Much blood has been spilt. Now it is time we can shed some tears, only then can this be washed away.

This vast country cannot feel the glow of freedom if power is concentrated in government secretariats. Millions and millions of our people in villages, towns and cities of India should have the responsibility of governing themselves. Ram Manohar Lohia and Jaya Prakash Narayan dreamt of decentralisation of power. We will fulfil their dreams. We shall bring forward legislation for genuine Panchayati Raj which will respect the imperatives of our federal structure.

Norms and values are the bedrock of democracy. Therefore, the sanctity of democratic institutions will be restored and the autonomy of the judiciary, CAG and Parliament will be strengthened.

We will establish a Lokpal to ensure that moral values of public life are not violated. Even the prime minister will not be above such scrutiny.

We will have to increase access to information. If the government functions in full public view, wrong doings will be minimised. To this end the Official Secrets Act will be amended and we will make the functioning of the government more transparent. Secrecy will be maintained only where the interests of national security and foreign relations so warrant.

Free flow of information is a prerequisite for democracy. The right to information will be enshrined in our Constitution and the Doordarshan and AIR will be given autonomy.

Inflation has hurt the poor. It is in these difficult circumstances that we have taken office. These difficulties will bring forth all our strength and resolution.

India lives in its villages. Today there is a flight of wealth, labour and talent from the villages. As long as these continue the villages will remain economically weak. We have resolved that at least half of the investment outlays should be channelled to the rural areas. The terms of trade for the farmers and workers have deteriorated and for their hard work they get debt and poverty. The small farmer, landless labourers, agricultural labourers, artisans and weavers will be provided with debt relief.

A very large number of scheduled caste and scheduled tribe brethren are without even basic shelter. It will be our primary aim to ensure that they lead lives of dignity and honour. The fire of hunger can be extinguished by food, but the fire that ignites the mind of the disinherited can only culminate in a revolution. History has placed on the agenda of the nation the imperative of economic and social justice. Life-long suffering is the fate of the weaker sections. Nothing is worse than a life of indignity. Social justice demands that hope must light up the lives of the weaker sections.

It will be our endeavour that minorities live without fear and as equal partners of our country's progress.

The future of the country depends on women; today they are neglected and exploited. The first step towards systematic change is to bring women into the national mainstream.

The youth has played a major role in the change of government. I am grateful to them. The youth of a nation are not called upon only to change the government; they are called upon to change history. Structures and systems are not changed in the corridors of power. Social forces have to be mobilised to transform society. I summon our youth to organise our people not only to change governments but also to bring about basic changes in the lives of the poor. Our democracy has to be liberated from the evil influence of money power. To this end, the youth can mobilise all working people in the struggle of a new order.

A country's foreign policy is built on the national consensus. Our policy of non-alignment derives from a national commitment. In the changed circumstances, we shall try to strengthen non-alignment. We shall continue to struggle for peace, disarmament and development. We are committed to fighting apartheid in South Africa and for securing the brave Palestinian people their inalienable rights. Effective steps will be taken to improve relations with our neighbours. It shall be our endeavour to make SAARC a dynamic institution.

I thank you for the support you have given for the change of the government. We need greater support for the work of the new government. We will give a government that every Indian will be proud of.

Jai Hind.

## Appendix II

# *First Press Conference*

*The prime minister addressed a press conference in New Delhi on 15 December 1989 within two weeks of assumption of office. The following excerpts are based on the transcript issued by the Press Information Bureau.*

Vishwanath Pratap Singh started the press conference with the following introductory remarks :

I want to put before you some of the major tasks before the government. The most important is restoration of democratic institutions, strengthening them and re-establishing their dignity. Taking the people into confidence and having an open government rather than one which puts the lid on facts and the truth. In this respect, we have already decided to bring forward the Lokpal bill this very session (of Parliament) on which three years were spent in the Select Committee.

Regarding autonomy to Doordarshan and AIR we are introducing a bill in this session.

Regarding declaration of assets (by ministers) a decision has been made and necessary enactment will be coming. Then, judicial reforms and electoral reforms; these are, as per our manifesto, high on our agenda. Then, strengthening of the federal structure, of relations between the Centre and the States. We propose to have an inter-State Council as has been envisaged in the Constitution.

Among the distortions that have taken place is the Posts and Telegraph Bill; we will withdraw it. Then, the fundamental rights. The right to life. In the fifty-ninth amendment (of the Constitution) it has been provided that the right to life will be taken away. We are committed to doing away with it. Then, strengthening and extending the democratisation process right to the grassroots level.

In this respect we will be bringing a panchayati raj bill. The opposition governments of Karnataka, West Bengal, Andhra Pradesh and Tamil Nadu, have established their models of panchayati raj. On these models we will be introducing legislation, but protecting the federal character of our Constitution. It will be our endeavour to involve voluntary organisations also. So, it becomes really a peoples' effort.

Industry will be given a positive boost because for a strong India we need a strong industrial base, particularly the small-scale sector, medium sector and agro-based industry.

Science and technology will be given special attention, particularly in the role of self-reliance which our scientists can play. There is tremendous potential of our scientists in this country. They have proved it so very often and we will give special attention to it.

On the economy we have made it clear that 50per cent of the total national resources of the Centre and the States combined would be committed to the rural areas.

Problems of youth and that of employment will be our topmost priorities. Special attention will be given to employment.

We have to see to the flow of investments into items of mass consumption. To contain price-rise over a long period is to ensure that items of mass consumption are adequately produced and there are no shortages on that account.

Regarding labour participation in management, we are committed to it. I have proposed that a discussion and seminar on labour participation in management involving the public sector and the various trade unions and people connected with it be held in first week of January.

Land reform is a very important area for the poor and for those who never reach the press or Delhi. To involve the chief ministers and to consider what improvements in law we can make on land records so that the poor really get land, we have enunciated in our National Front manifesto that legislation regarding land reforms would be placed in the ninth schedule of the Constitution so that litigation is limited and undue money and time of the poor are not taken away.

Regarding economy, we are faced with a situation which is causing a lot of concern to us and we have asked the Economic Advisory Council which is headed by Sukhomoy Chakravarty to prepare a white paper regarding it. So, the bench-mark is there to determine at what stage we are starting and what the problems are.

Answering a question whether the Bofors enquiry is proceeding according to expectation, the prime minister said:

I have made it very clear that the law will have its course and there is no question of either diluting it or, on the other hand, being vindictive about it. So we have not to err this way or that way. What the law dictates, we will implement and we will review all the issues which were under debate during the last few years.

Q: Mr. Prime Minister, you have said that the law of the land will take its course while dealing with the Bofors issue. How would it be different than the law of this land and the laws of those countries which are involved in this deal? How do you intend to pursue the case? What is the time frame?

PM: What do you exactly mean by this?

Q: Because on Bofore issue you have said that the law of the land will take its course.

PM: Yes.

Q: Law of which land?

PM: India.

Q: But the Bofors issue involves laws of other lands.

PM: We can enforce our laws.

Q: The National Front spokesman has said that once you form the government, within one month you will get the names. Will you be able to get them in one month or six weeks?.

PM: I have told you exactly what we are going to do. We are going to enforce the law.

Q: The question is not whether you are going to see that the law of the land takes its course. It is 13 days since you have been sworn in. What we want to know is, have you initiated any process? *The Hindu* newspaper reported from Geneva that the Swiss authorities are just waiting for a telefax message from your government to say that the money put in the secret accounts of that country should be frozen because it is illegal. We want to know what you have done about it. You have been saying that the law of the land will take its course. It will have to take its course. But what have you done so far?

PM: I do not think you will be dissatisfied with our action.

Q: Mr. Prime Minister, you have mentioned briefly about Jammu & Kashmir and Punjab. I am aware of some of the things which you are doing on that. You have called an all-party conference on Punjab on Sunday. Could you give us a little more details about how you plan to attack these two quite serious problems?

PM: I think, even before the details, what is more important is to generate the atmosphere. Many a time many an initiative is lost; while the details are all very good, but the atmosphere is not right. So, our first attempt is to create a proper atmosphere, and it is in this light that we are making a national effort trying to involve every section because it is not a question of one party but of the country.

Q: Mr. Prime Minister, when we travel in the troubled areas of the country, people invariably give two reasons for their growing alienation. One is the large-scale military presence that makes them feel under occupation and the second is, what they say, the political use of intelligence agencies. In your future dealings with the States, what will be your policy with the States? Will it be a policy of proper use of military and para-military and also the intelligence agencies?

PM: You know, precisely for this very reason, whatever may be the apprehensions in the minds of people, I removed all security (restrictions) while moving in Amritsar and, I think, that gives the proper signal as to the spirit in which we want to approach the problem.

Q: Mr. Prime Minister, you have given, apparently, a very high priority to freedom of the media, autonomy to Doordarshan and Radio. I would like to know whether you are thinking of a new media policy which, I believe, is already in the works of the I & B Ministry. I also want to know whether you are going to look at the problems that the industry is facing, like newsprint and freedom of getting more and more information accurately.

P.I.O. We will go from topic to topic and, I think, that will be easier. We will first finish with the subject of Punjab and Kashmir.

Q: Mr. Prime Minister, an impression has been created by some of your actions in the last few days that just to keep your minority government in power, you are prepared to compromise with terrorism and communalism. Do you like to dispel the impression?

PM: It is a minority government with majority support. But I want to make it clear that there is no question of compromise with the territory of the country or any partitioning of the country. At the same time, the approach to the problem cannot be mechanical and cannot be solely confined to administrative measures or the administrative machinery. It has to be addressed to the people because it is from there that final solutions will come.

Q: Mr. Prime Minister, I want to ask two questions on Punjab. Number one, in the proposed all-party meeting on Punjab would you like to involve all sections of the Akali Dal or only the Mann group?

PM: We would like to involve all sections.

Q: Another question: Would you discuss the Rajiv-Sant Longowal accord at the proposed meeting and do you feel that implementation of the accord in toto can bring peace to Punjab?

PM: It is an open agenda. Anything that can lead to a solution, we will discuss.

Q: We have conflicting reports about the role of the Jammu and Kashmir Government in the recent episode. According to one account, they did what they ought to have done. They were correct. According to another, they dragged their feet on crucial occasions. Now, what exactly is the Centre's view and how does the Centre propose to go about it? There has been a demand for drastic action like dismissal of the Government, change of Governor, etc. What is your thinking here?

PM: We are reviewing the whole situation. To be fair to the J &K government, we have asked the chief minister also to come here. We will assess the whole situation. But we are not in favour of any precipitate action, because it is a very delicate situation there.

Q: The situation in Punjab and Kashmir is serious. But there is also serious violence in other States. For example in, Andhra Pradesh, Naxalites are ruling half the State. Are you going to have an integrated approach to this problem? That kind of violence is spreading from Punjab to Telengana, Telengana to Andhra. Are you going to have an integrated approach to meet this violence?

PM: I think it is a very pertinent question you have asked. In fact, violence was not in our political ethos and it is a new development for us and it is being used increasingly in various forms. Even in elections, we saw in the last elections, it has penetrated the electoral process. An integrated view on this matter will have to be taken. I think the National Integration Council will be the forum where we could come together and address ourselves to this problem.

Q: Because of the permission given for the Ramshila procession and later on, the laying of the foundation stone at Ayodhya, by the previous Government, we have seen what happened in the country during the elections; the chain of communal riots in various parts of the country. Now, I want to ask you, if there is no decision by the Allahabad High Court and if you are not able to arrive at an agreed solution before the assembly election, will you ban further activity, construction activity, at the site so that the Assembly elections can take place in an atmosphere not surcharged by communal passion and tension?

PM: There are too many 'ifs' in your question.

We are for an amicable solution of this issue. I do feel there are possibilities of an amicable solution and we will establish a dialogue. I have not given up hope. Of course, the processes of the courts are there.

Q: In the 16 priorities of the new government listed by you I did not find a mention of communal harmony. The Babri Masjid and other demands have been raised. The VHP has almost given you an ultimatum day-before-yesterday. Also, there have been questions raised about Mathura and other issues. Is there any comprehensive policy or plan with the government to solve this question of communal disharmony in the country?

Communal harmony is our topmost priority. Even in the election campaign, which is a political process, it was the very first item that we used to mention and the country's strength lies in its emotional unity and integrity. It will be our endeavour to maintain and strengthen the same. So, sometimes certain things do not make news, but they are much more basic than news. I think communal harmony is much more basic and it is the underlined subject of our all efforts.

Q: Will you include the BJP and CPM in the government?

PM: You know the position that they are extending support from outside. When it is from outside, how can it be inside?

Q: But Mr. Devi Lal has been talking about efforts to take them into the government.

PM: I am stating the facts (Interruptions). They have made their position very clear.

Q: Mr. George Fernandes has categorically said that Pepsi Cola has to go. What is your government's policy? Are you going to throw out Pepsi Cola?

PM: We will certainly look into the terms of their participation, and also take an overall view of the confidence of those who would like to invest in India. So within these two parameters, we will have a look at it.

Q: The press pool of housing for journalists has come under attack for the second time in 1988. First it came under attack in 1976 but the distortion was set right by the Janata government in the very first few days. The second distortion has taken place in 1988 and the press pool of housing for journalists is being phased out and eliminated. The facility was given by the government because it was found to be essential. Would you like to commit in principle that the distortion will be removed and there will be restoration of the facility for the press in the capital?

PM: We will review this. Journalists are an essential part of democracy and in a democracy they have to be housed, anyway.

Q: I have rolled two issues into one the mounting deficit and the debt trap, internal and external. Would you enact a law to limit government borrowing as recommended by the Public Accounts Committee in 1962?

PM: I think this is a very pertinent question, a relevant question. I think we should bring it into focus, debate on it because we are faced with deficit which then leads to borrowing or printing of money. I will not immediately today spell out a solution. But I very much share your concern. And there is need for taking very concrete steps to restrain the government from violating financial norms. There are practical difficulties in it. It is not possible for me to spell them now. But certainly it is in our mind as to how we do find a restraint in the system itself on this matter.

Q: Your government has said that it will correct the imbalance between direct and indirect taxes. Does it mean that the direction set by your 1985 budget was wrong?

PM: If you remember that, well, it is not my budget. It is always the budget of the government. I do not carry personal budgets with me. But, anyway, even then, if you see, there was the maximum rise of revenue from direct taxes. Forty-five per cent increase was achieved in the personal income-tax and twenty-three per cent, I think, overall. So, there was correction of that because more revenue came from direct taxes.

Q: You have come to power on the promise of controlling and bringing down the prices. What are your short-term measures to bring down the prices of essential commodities?

PM: Our short-term measures get neutralised by the long-term measures taken earlier. Money circulation is high. The rate is between 18 and 19 per cent, and that is causing a general pressure on prices.

When you know that money is pumped, it is not one day's affair to set the position right. It takes time. Production matches the money supply and then you reduce it over a period of time. But certainly we shall take some measures and in the short time we are hopeful that it will have its impact. But our major problem is that of large deficits, increased money supply and in this macro-management you know it is no use painting rosy pictures. We hope over a period of time we will be able to correct the distortions.

Q: You are now unaware that a large business house has used the financial institutions to buy up a company. There are also two reports of a committee set up by the government. The Grover Committee report has been lying unrevealed. When are you going to release these reports and take follow up action on them?

PM: Each issue has to be decided on its merits. So, it is not possible for me to pick up one case and tell you what is going to be done. But whatever is fair under the provisions of the law will be followed.

Q: You have come to power on the promise that you will not encourage dynastic rule. But your deputy prime minister has a flourishing dynasty in Haryana. Comment.

PM: Well, in a democratic setup the final decision is with the people and the representatives of the people.

Q: Will your Government reopen the Indira Gandhi assassination case, or, at least, publish the annexures to the Thakkar Commission's report and the special investigative team's report? This was the demand of the opposition which the previous government refused to concede.

PM: We made that demand. Now, we will implement it.

Q: You are going to introduce a bill on autonomy for Doordarshan in this session (of Parliament). But the process of that becoming law will take about six months. What will happen in the interim period?

PM: The law will be expedited but you cannot expect the law to expedite. The spirit will be implemented even before the law is finally crystallised.

Q: One of your election planks was eradication of corruption of the previous regime. Will you resort to a raid raj and penalise people who were encouraged to generate black money because of the previous government's policy? Secondly, how are you going to cleanse the system which promotes generation of black money?

PM: Generation of black money. We have very clearly said in our Front manifesto that we will take all steps so that generation of black money is curbed. The steps will have to be both administrative and economic measures. Only administrative measures cannot fully cope with it. So, economic measures will have to be taken.

About raids, there cannot be animus against anyone or any particular person or any particular group and I want to dispel apprehensions of motivated action. So, while there will be no such things, I cannot also grant immunity to those who violate the law. If they violate the law, they will have to face the full rigour of the law.

Q: Will you give a fresh cut-off date?

PM: Cut-off date for what?

Q: Those people who were evading taxes during the previous regime and those helped by the previous government. Will you give them a fresh cut-off date?

PM: I do not understand what is a cut-off date?

Q: Certain policies of the previous regime led to tax evasion. Are you going to penalise those people or will you give them a fresh cut-off date?

PM: There is no cut-off date for violation of the law.

Q: My question is about the politicalisation of government machinery in the past five years. Ever since Mr. Rajiv Gandhi became the prime minister, there was a systematic and appalling misuse of the intelligence and investigative agencies to further the needs of the Congress party. The witch-hunt was carried to several foreign countries, as you know, with the help of some opposition politicians and established journalists. Since your government has come to power promising an open society, will you take early steps to tell the full truth to the people in this regard through a comprehensive white paper?

PM: I will assure you that we will keep the bureaucracy, or their work confined to what they are responsible for under the Constitution and not involve them in any political activity. I think that would be a very good corrective to whatever may have happened. Certainly, we are an open government, we will bring it to light, but we have to give positive backing to upright, honest and efficient officers and give them responsibility. That will be one of the things which will be in our mind.

Q: You first fell out with Rajiv Gandhi because you hired the Fairfax agency to investigate economic crimes. Now as prime minister would you again favour hiring of foreign agencies to investigate criminal activities?

PM: One has to go by the merits of the case and in the overall context. Unless there is a specific case, it is not possible to give a general answer.

Q: From what the finance minister recently said about liquidation of debts, we got the impression that it will not be possible for your government to write off all loans because of empty coffers, as you once put it, that you have inherited from the previous government. What have you to say, would you be able to fulfil the pledge given to the people?

PM: With the financial condition that we have inherited it is a very difficult situation. I think the finance minister was expresing that concern, but it is also a question of our credibility. So, when we have to meet the promise, we will find the means to fulfil it.

Q: The Sri Lankan foreign minister has said that he has conveyed two urgent requests to you. One that India should honour its commitment and withdraw all its troops by December 31. And the second is that the Tamil National Army which is said to have been illegally created, trained and armed by the IPKF should be disbanded because the Tamil National Army is fighting Sri Lankan security forces and rival Tamil groups. What is your government's thinking on these two requests conveyed to you by Mr. Vijeyratne?

PM: On this issue we have made ourselves clear. Of course, we have inherited a situation. It is not that we are starting with a clean slate. And we cannot wish away a ground reality which is there today. Mr. Vijeyratne had come here. We did tell him that we would want to work jointly on the de-induction of troops and we made our intention clear that we would expedite it. But it would require cooperation from the Sri Lankan government also. And he agreed to a joint working of the de-induction. At the same time, lives of the Tamil population, also their safety and security, has to be ensured and there are certain aspirations of the people there, of devolution and democratic aspirations. So all have to be ensured.

Q: What about TNA?

PM: Well, there is a citizens' volunteer force and we are in dialogue with the Sri Lankan Government on the various problems between us. I think at this stage it will be better to keep things at that level.

Q: Will the IPKF be withdrawn completely by the end of this month?

PM: Well, I have told you that we are committed. The Indian and the Sri Lankan governments are committed to work jointly for expeditious de-induction of the forces.

Q: Does this mean that the troops will not be withdrawn until power is devolved to the Tamil community?

PM: When I said this, I was expressing the aspirations of the people there. Regarding de-induction, I said that we have to work jointly.

Q: This question relates to one of the portfolios that you hold,*i.e.* defence. In recent days, Pakistan has been holding one of its biggest military exercises. On the other hand for the past, I think, two years, the Indian defence budget has been frozen, with the result that the operational readiness and the sustainability of the Indian armed forces have been seriously affected. Does your government plan to do anything about this?

PM: Regarding the military exercise, it is one of the biggest exercises that Pakistan has ever done. However, at DGMO level, both the countries are in contact. Yes, the resources crunch affects the defence budget also and while certainly we do not want any wasteful expenditure that may be in the defence area, at the same time we cannot compromise with our security. Many a time, the defence budget has to respond to threats across the border. So the compulsions of the defence budget come many a time from outside the country and it also shares the overall financial situation in the budget. Certainly we cannot make compromises on security and while on development, resources have to be met, on this side at least the minimum has to be maintained.

Q: Your breach with the former prime minister came on the West German submarine deal. You started inquiring and you were out of office. Now that you are not only the prime minister but also the defence minister, have you reopened the inquiry?

PM: We are reviewing all aspects in these matters.

Q: We have just witnessed the most acute anti-Indian demonstration in Kashmir since you took over and, obviously, the demonstrators are very pro-Pakistan. Could I also ask you about the easy release of the terrorists? Is this a policy of your government or was it a special gesture made because she the hostage is the home minister's daughter?

PM: No, it could have been anyone's daughter, and it was a very special circumstance. But it is not a general policy. And there is no question of compromise with the country's sovereignty or compromise with any force that challenges the sovereignty of the country. At the same time, I think there are a lot of problems at the people's level in J & K--the problems of the youth, employment and development of Jammu and Kashmir. I think they have to be gone into deeply and addressed to. And here also comes the issue of emotional integration and I think we should tackle it in a very deft way with flexibility.

Q: The very same senior bureaucrats whom your party colleagues had earlier accused of misusing their official position to project the former ruling party, are today running your government, or else, have been given prestigious posts abroad. Would you like to comment?

PM: Officials run the government which is in power.

Q: In your first broadcast to the nation, there was no mention of Mahatma Gandhi. Was it an inadvertent omission or part of ideological reflection of the new government?

PM: How can anyone forget Father of the Nation?

Q: You talked about empty coffers. Do you intend to go in for a loan from the IMF and, if so, will this not hamper the implementation of your policies because of the conditionalities of the IMF?

PM: The balance of payments situation, as I said, does cause us concern. But, with resolute action--and there will be need for resolute actions on that front--we can steer clear of the debt trap.

And it will be too early, at this stage, to define the exact course, but I think we will have to take the country into confidence as to what state of affairs the last government has brought the country to on this issue. But, I am sure, with the cooperation of the people, not only for benefits from the government--they are for the independence of the country and its economic independence--we will share the struggle in this respect.

Q: About India's important role in the non-aligned movement, should we expect that under your leadership you would like to strengthen the NAM? And secondly, what role India, under your leadership, will play to strengthen relations with the Arab world and to bring permanent peace in the Gulf, between Iraq and Iran and Lebanon?

PM: Foreign policy is not partisan. I mean, it does not belong to a single party. It is dictated by geopolitical considerations. And it is also the result of a national consensus. I think the policy of non-alignment has evolved through a process of national consensus, and it has served the interests of the country. We will pursue it and strengthen it. And the elements of our non-alignment have been our solidarity with the developing countries, our friendship with the Arab countries, commitment to the Palestinian cause and our opposition to apartheid. So, these elements of our foreign policy will continue.

Q: People of this country are very much concerned about the stability of your government, and in this connection they are anxious to know whether you have resolved your differences with Mr. Chandra Shekhar and whether you will invite him to join your government.

PM: About internal matters of the party I do not express myself in the press. But we are in full co-operation. Today on the Punjab and Kashmir issues I have asked Chandra Shekharji to participate in the discussions. I will request him to participate in the discussions on the 17th. So, I think the basis of your question does not remain. Of course, opinion in a democracy ... what the country has paid, let me express myself. The country has paid much more heavily because of dead silence in terms of national interest and in terms of decay of democratic institutions. And I think, we should never cultivate that cult. Let us not put political unity on a pedestal under which democracy itself is crushed. Many tomb-stones of democracy bear the inscription "Unity".

Q: The National Front election manifesto mentions that the 1985 Assam accord will be faithfully implemented. You have also promised special attention to the north-eastern States to tackle their various problems. My question is: How do you propose to tackle the problems of the north-eastern States? What is going to be done about Assam's problems, especially the problem of violence by a section of the Bodo people?

PM: I understand the importance of the North-Eastern problem. That is why one of my first visits will be to Assam and the north-east.

Q: The chief election commissioner has spoken of the previous government's record of violating electoral decencies and ethics. What checks and balances your government would adopt in order not to interfere with the functioning of the election commission and would you continue with the two new election commissioners appointed just before the elections, who were charged with subverting the electoral process?

PM: We will come with a whole package of electoral reforms, which will include the election commission. Regarding your question on specific appointments etc., we will review it.

Q: You had once said and I quote: "I will be disaster as a prime minister." Do you still hold that view, or do you regret having said it?

PM: You still risk that danger.

Q: The government of Nepal has offered fresh negotiations on the trade dispute. What is your government's response to that?

PM: We will enter into a dialogue.

Q: Pakistan has proposed a number of steps for further normalisation of relations between the two countries including those relating to nuclear non-proliferation and the issue of armed forces of the two countries. What is your response to it?

PM: Well, I think, it is not only a bilateral issue. It is a global issue. We cannot take it only in one context. But we have spelt out our own position on this issue. Peaceful uses of nuclear energy. It is not only ourselves but the whole world should move in this direction. This has been our consistent stand. But there are many areas where positive steps could be taken in improving the relations with Pakistan. Economic field, in the area of trade, in the area of economic co-operation and of exchange and travel; these are areas where, certainly, improvement in relations could be made.

Q: There is a fear among the Congress ruled states that the Centre may dismiss them. Would you like to say something about it?

PM: It is the people who dismiss.

Q: There is a feeling among the neighbouring countries that the perception that India was a regional bully would be dispelled. But your remarks on Sri Lanka seem to emphasise on continuity rather than change. Would you like to comment?

PM: I want to make it very clear. Our approach to the neighbouring countries will be one of friendliness, no any arm-twisting or any bullying tactics. I want to make this clear. Strength lies in mutual understanding.

Q: How do you view the role of Pakistan in giving support, be it military or moral to the extremists in Kashmir?

PM: I think, there were many statements from Pakistan condemning the kidnapping. Whenever we come across any incident, we express our concern and our reservations. But I note that Pakistan has given an assurance that they will not encourage extremists and, I think, the assurance given to us will be fulfilled.

Q: Positive developments are taking place now in the international sphere and one of the most important has been the Soviet-American summit in Malta. I would like to know, what is the position of your government on the major international issues such as disarmament and development. And, what can you say about the prospects of Indo-Soviet co-operation?

PM: On disarmament and development, it is our commitment to both these goals and we very much welcome the initiatives that have been taken by Mr. Gorbachev and the equally good response from the US, by President Bush. I think it will go a long way in removing the barriers of suspicion and mistrust. It is something positive which the world is looking to. There is still a long way to go. But I think it has come as a new reality. We welcome this development.

As for the USSR, it has been our traditional friend and we will continue our policy of strengthening our friendship with the USSR and co-operation in many fields. There are possibilities, not only in strengthening, but new possibilities of co-operation in various fields.

Q: According to the blue book the prime minister is entitled to a fleet of three helicopters for campaigning while the opposition leaders have to travel by cars as you did last month. Do you want to change it before the next Assembly elections?

PM: In electoral reforms all these would be reviewed. Let us see how it comes.

Appendix III

# The Action Plan

The manifesto of the National Front has presented a concrete programme of action. Ministries and departments have been requested to identify priority areas of action for implementation in a time-bound manner. The first set of points on which the action is underway is listed below. Ministries and departments will prepare comprehensive and detailed action plans on these and other items and announce them separately. Implementation of the action plans will be a matter of highest priority and will be closely monitored.

An outlay of at least 50% of investible resources in the agricultural and rural sectors of the economy will be ensured starting with the Annual Plan for 1990-91.

In order to give the farmers a remunerative price for their produce, the following changes are being made in the method of computing support prices:

(i) Introduce a formula for adjusting support prices for inflation from the date of announcement to the time of market.

(ii) Labour will be costed on the basis of actual wages paid or minimum wages, whichever is higher, instead of the present system where it is costed on the basis of actual wages paid when there are lower than the minimum wages.

(iii) Include an element of managerial or entrepreneurial labour in the family labour input and cost this labour at the higher rate than agricultural labour.

The ministry of agriculture will appoint an expert committee to recommend ways of implementing these changes and their recommendation will be taken into account in fixing prices for the next kharif season.

"The right to work" will be made a fundamental right and the necessary Bill for amending the Constitution will be introduced in the forthcoming budget session. An employment guarantee scheme will be implemented progressively.

A comprehensive Constitutional amendment bill on panchayati raj will be prepared and introduced during the budget session of Parliament, after discussion with the chief ministers.

The government places the highest importance on land reforms. All land reforms legislation will be incorporated in the ninth schedule to the Constitution. Land Reforms will continue to be on the agenda in the proposed Inter-State Council. A meeting of the chief ministers will be held by April, 1990 to finalise a programme of land reforms implementation.

A scheme for debt relief up to Rs. 10,000 to small, marginal and landless cultivators and artisans will be finalised during the forthcoming budget session.

A long term fiscal policy will be presented during the budget session.

The government is committed to curbing ostentatious and elitist consumption and the measures required in this regard will be taken early.

With a view to pushing up exports in a big way and plugging loopholes in the import-export rules and simplifying the procedures.

(i) A new three year import-export policy will be announced on 1 - 4 -1990.

(ii) Simplified pre-shipment documentation will be finalised and announced on 1 - 3 - 1990.

(iii) Export policy will encourage the export of items with high net foreign exchange content.

The ministry of defence shall appoint a Committee to examine modalities for implementing a scheme for realising the National Front's commitment to the principle of "one rank one pension" for ex-servicemen. The Committee will submit its report by 31-3-1990.

A national security council under the chairmanship of prime minister will be set up by April, 1990.

A comprehensive bill on electoral reforms will be introduced in the budget session of Parliament.

A high level judicial commission will be set up for appointments and transfers of judges. The necessary Constitutional amendment bill is proposed to be introduced in the budget session.

A bill to amend the Legal Services Authorities Act will be introduced in the budget session with a view to strengthening Lok Adalats and legal aid programmes.

A bill for setting up an autonomous corporation for TV and Radio has already been introduced on 29th December, 1989. It is proposed to have the Bill enacted after a national debate during the budget session.

The government will, by amending the Constitution, guarantee the 'right to information' as a fundamental right. The bill for the purpose will be introduced during the budget session.

New bills will be brought in during the budget session to amend the Indian Post Office Act and the Indian Telegraph Act, ensuring that the citizen's right to privacy is respected. The Indian Post Office (Amendment) Bill, 1986 will be withdrawn.

The National Integration Council for reviewing issues relating to national integration, and to make recommendations thereon will be reconstituted. A meeting of chief ministers to consider this matter will be held in January, 1990. The proposal in this regard will be finalised thereafter and the first meeting of the Council convened before April, 1990.

An amendment of the Official Secrets Act to ensure the citizen's right to information will be carried out. A bill for this purpose will be introduced in the budget session.

An inter-State Council will be set up after the forthcoming elections to the legislative assemblies of the States. The process of eliciting the views of the State governments on the nature of duties to be performed by the inter-State Council, and its organisation and procedures, will be started straightaway.

Special measures under a 15-point programme for minorities will be formulated during the budget session of Parliament to ensure for minorities adequate implementation of development programmes, representation in employment, enhanced availability of credit and increased facilities for technical education.

A committee will be set up before the end of January, 1990 to examine the recommendations of the Gujral Committee.

A scheme to ensure that special csourts are promptly set up for expeditious disposal of cases relating to caste and communal riots and atrocities will be finalised before March, 1990

The Prevention of Atrocities Act for prevention of atrocities against members of the scheduled castes and scheduled tribes, which is still to be notified, will be made effective by 31st January, 1990 after a meeting with State governments.

A cabinet committee will be set up in January, 1990 for consideration of the recommendations of the second Backward Classes Commission (Mandal Commission).

Promotion of workers' participation in the management of industries will be given high priority. A national seminar is being organised for this purpose during January, 1990 and further steps will be worked out by the end of February, 1990. Necessary legislation will be brought up during the budget session of Parliament.

A new industrial relations bill will be brought forward during the monsoon session of Parliament, and necessary consultations with all the interests will be completed before the end of May, 1990.

Substantial expansion of the existing programmes serving the urban poor will be undertaken from April, 1990.

(i) Provision of basic services and facilities in slums, with particular attention to the needs of women and children.

(ii) A significantly stepped up scheme for providing night shelter for pavement dwellers in major cities; it is hoped to benefit about one lakh persons during 1990-91.

(iii) A comprehensive national housing policy for different sections of society, with specific programmes directed towards the poor, and improving the housing finance system, to be finalised during the budget session of Parliament.

(iv) Liberation and rehabilitation of scavengers in medium and small towns according to a time-bound programme covering 500 towns annually.

A master plan for providing a network of warehouses and godowns, both in public and co-operative sectors, for the entire country will be drawn up by 31st March, 1990 to insure farmers against distress sale.

A long term policy on licensing of sugar mills will be announced by 31st March, 1990 to eliminate political favouritism and bureaucratic arbitrariness.

A commission on women will be set up to ensure due representation of women in all spheres, to check discrimination, for enforcement of the rights of women and redressal of their grievances. This will be set up by the budget session.

An all india conference of youth leaders will be convened by March, 1990 to chalk out a programme of involvement of youth in nation building.

The science & technology programmes will be reviewed to provide emphasis on the needs of rural society, especially in the areas of poverty alleviation, water management and land use.

A review of our environmental policy and laws, especially as they affect the tribal population, will be undertaken to ensure that our twin objectives of protection of tribal interests and protection of our environment are pursued in a harmonious manner, by April 1990.

# Index